Discovering Cyprus in 2024

From the Heart of… Greece, Limassol, The Paphos, Augustina, Mountains of Troodos and Les Arcs

All rights reserved. No part of this publication may be reproduced, distributed, or transmitted in any form or by any means, including photocopying, recording, or other electronic or mechanical methods, without the prior written permission of the publisher, except in the case of brief quotations embodied in critical reviews and certain other noncommercial uses permitted by copyright law.
Copyright ©Alice Lundy,2024.

TABLE OF CONTENT

Chapter 1
    Overview of Cyprus
    Synopsis of Cyprus
    The Past and Present
    Climate and Geography

Chapter 2
    Making Travel Plans
    When to Go There
    Entry and Visa Requirements
    Money and Finance

Chapter 3
    Traveling to Cyprus
    Aircraft and Airports
    Points of Entry

Chapter 4
    Recommendations
    Resorts and Hotels
    Low-Cost Lodging
    Outdoor and Camping Provisions

Chapter 5
    Regions and Cities of Cyprus
    Greece
    Limassol
    The Paphos
    Les Arcs
    Augustina
    Mountains of Troodos

Chapter 6
- Leading Attractions and Monuments
- Archaeological Sites and Ancient Ruins
- Water Sports and Beaches
- Cultural Centers and Museums
- Natural Attractions and Parks

Chapter 7
- Sports and Entertainment
- Exploration of Nature and Hiking
- After Dark and Entertainment
- Markets and shopping

Chapter 8
- Food and Dining
- Greek Cooking
- Customary Recipes
- Well-liked Cafes and Restaurants

Chapter 9
- Regional Events and Customs
- Holidays and Religion
- Conventional Dance and Music
- Spoken Word and Listening

Chapter 10
- Relevant Information
- Travel Advice and Safety
- Regional Laws and Traditions
- Handy Expressions & Linguistic Advice

Chapter 11
- Moving About

    The Public Transit System
    Car Hire
Chapter 12
    Taking Families and Kids on Vacation
    Activities Suitable for the Whole Family
    Health and Child Care Services
Chapter 13
    Outdoor Excursions
    Snorkeling and Scuba Pursuit
    Using a Kite and Windsurfer
    Hiking and Climbing Rocks
Chapter 14
    Traveling With Caution
    Greenhouse Gas Initiatives
    Conscientious Travel Approaches
Chapter 15
    Emergency Contacts and Resources
    Value-Added Phone Numbers
    Missions Abroad and Consulates
    Healthcare Institutions
Chapter 16
    Addenda
    Maps and Schedules of Transportation
    Linguistic Translation Reference
Chapter 17
    Index
    Instantaneous Keyword Index

Chapter 1

Overview of Cyprus

Situated in the center of the Mediterranean, Cyprus is a magnificent island that entices tourists with an intriguing fusion of culture, history, and scenic splendor. Cyprus offers an enthralling adventure for any traveler, with a history spanning millennia and a scenery that varies from sun-drenched beaches to harsh highlands. It is a welcoming location for anyone looking for both adventure and relaxation because of its mild Mediterranean environment, welcoming residents, and rich tapestry of historical legends. Welcome to a place where history and modernity coexist and where exploration abounds around every corner.

Synopsis of Cyprus

Cyprus is a fascinating island that connects Europe and Asia, and it is located in the eastern Mediterranean. Because of its advantageous location, it has always been a mingling pot of cultures and influences. This island nation has a lot to offer, from gorgeous beaches and clear oceans to a rich cultural past. Its food is a unique fusion of Greek and Turkish flavors, and you may tour quaint villages with tiny cobblestone alleys and historic ruins that tell stories of previous civilizations. The geological diversity of the island is also remarkable, offering adventure seekers mountains, woods, and immaculate coasts. With its pleasant environment, Cyprus is a popular vacation spot for sun worshippers as well as for those who want to explore the wonders of history and become fully immersed in a friendly and lively culture.

The Past and Present

The history and culture of Cyprus are interwoven with the Mediterranean like fine threads. The history of this island is a complex synthesis of influences from many ancient cultures, including the Ottomans, Greeks, Romans, and Byzantines. Because of its advantageous location, it has been sought after by numerous dynasties, leaving a legacy of varied customs and architectural styles.

The island is renowned for its distinctive blend of cultures in addition to its historical significance. The two groups of Cypriots, Greek and Turkish, live on the same island but have different languages, traditions, and religious customs. Due to this duality, Cyprus has developed into a unique cultural mosaic where visitors can experience both Greek and Turkish customs. Warm hospitality, delectable food, traditional music, and dances that honor the island's colorful past are characteristics of the native Cypriot culture. Discovering historic historical sites, meandering through quaint towns, or indulging in authentic Cypriot cuisine are just a few of the ways that Cyprus's rich history and culture will enrich and contextualize your trip. It is a location where the past and current coexist peacefully, offering visitors a singular and immersive cultural experience.

Climate and Geography

Climate and Geography:

The island of Cyprus, which is in the eastern Mediterranean, is remarkably diverse. The island's varied terrain, which offers visitors a multitude of experiences, varies from rocky highlands to coastal plains. One notable feature is the Troodos Mountains, which are located in the island's western region. In addition to being breathtakingly beautiful, these mountains provide a more refreshing respite from the summertime heat of the Mediterranean. The Troodos are dotted with several hiking trails, beautiful forests, and quaint settlements. On the other side, tourists are primarily drawn to Cyprus's shoreline. The island's coastline areas provide golden sand beaches and pristine waters that are ideal for swimming, sunbathing, and water sports. Particularly the southern shore is well-known for its hospitable beaches. Cyprus has a year-round climate; the summer months are popular with sun worshippers, while the cooler months are great for visiting historical monuments and engaging in outdoor activities without the strong heat.

Impact on Your Trip:

It's critical to comprehend Cyprus's topography and climate when organizing your vacation. The time of year may influence the destinations and activities you choose. Summertime is the best time of year for beachgoers, but it can get busy. Because of their cooler temperatures, spring and autumn are great seasons for outdoor activities and cultural exploration. You can better plan by looking at the weather prediction for the dates of your particular trip. Cyprus is a year-round destination due to its varied topography and pleasant Mediterranean climate, which suit a variety of travel interests, whether you're looking to unwind by the beaches, go trekking in the highlands, or explore historical monuments.

Chapter 2

Making Travel Plans

Choose a season that best fits your tastes when organizing your trip to Cyprus. Summers in the Mediterranean region are long and sunny, which is ideal for beachgoers and those who enjoy water activities. But if you'd rather go outside in nicer weather with fewer people around, spring and autumn make excellent seasons for seeing historical sites and engaging in outdoor activities. Cyprus offers something to offer any kind of traveler, whether they are looking for an energetic vacation, a cultural experience, or a laid-back beach vacation.

When to Go There

When to Go to Cyprus: Travelers may find something to do all year round in Cyprus thanks to its varied attractions and Mediterranean environment. The ideal time to go will primarily rely on your travel plans and areas of interest.

1. Summer:
- June through August: Perfect for sun enthusiasts. The island's stunning beaches are the ideal place to relax due to the hot, dry weather. Swimming, snorkeling, and windsurfing are among the most popular water sports. But since it's the busiest travel time of year, popular spots could be packed and lodging costs could be higher.

2. Spring (March to May) and Autumn (September to November):
- These transitional seasons are great options if you want warmer temperatures and fewer crowds. Cyprus is especially beautiful in the spring when the country is a riot of wildflowers and verdant scenery. It's the perfect season for going on hikes, touring historical places, and taking advantage of outdoor activities without the oppressive heat.

3. Winter (December to February):

- Although Cyprus doesn't have a hard winter, these are the months when it can get wetter and colder, particularly in the mountains. Winter might be a serene time to visit the island if you want to explore cultural sights at your leisure and avoid the summer crowds.

The season you choose should suit your style of travel. Think about the pursuits you want to engage in and the weather that you find comfortable. Cyprus is a place that can be enjoyed all year round because it provides a distinct experience regardless of the season.

Entry and Visa Requirements

Requirements for Entry and Visas:

Depending on your nationality and the reason for your visit, you may need to take into account the necessary documents for admission and a visa when visiting Cyprus. To help you in making travel plans, below is a broad overview:

1. **Visa-Free Travel:**
   - Nationals of the European Union (EU), the European Economic Area (EEA), and numerous other nations, including the US, Canada, Australia, and many more, are not required to obtain a visa to enter Cyprus for brief stays, often lasting up to 90 days. It is advised to visit the official Cyprus government website or get in touch with the closest Cypriot embassy or consulate for up-to-date information, as admission criteria are subject to change.

2. **Validity of Passport:**
   - Verify that your passport is still valid three months after the day you want to leave Cyprus. To prevent any issues, it's usually a good idea to have additional validity.

3. **Extended Visits and Particular Objectives:**
   - A visa or residency permit can be required if you intend to stay in Cyprus for a longer amount of time or particular objectives, such as employment or study. It is advised to contact the embassy or

the appropriate Cypriot authorities for detailed information and application procedures, as the requirements for extended visits can be more complicated.

4. Travel Insurance:

- Having all-inclusive travel insurance that covers medical expenses and other unforeseen circumstances is a good idea.

5. Customs Rules:

- To guarantee a seamless arrival, familiarize yourself with Cyprus's customs rules. Know what goods you are allowed to import and what you are not.

Please be aware that admission criteria could change based on your citizenship as well as the dynamic nature of the diplomatic and political landscape. Before departing for Cyprus, it is imperative to confirm the most recent visa and entry requirements. To ensure a hassle-free visit to this stunning Mediterranean island, always plan and make sure you have the required paperwork.

Money and Finance

Cyprus's banking and currency:

Comprehending the Cyprus currency and financial system is crucial for an effortless journey to this island in the Mediterranean. What you should know is as follows:

Currency:

- The Euro (EUR) is the accepted form of payment in Cyprus. It is simple to manage daily transactions because it is denominated in both coins and banknotes. The majority of shops, lodging facilities, and dining establishments on the island take Euro payments. Having some cash on hand is a good idea for modest purchases, particularly in less visited or rural locations.

Banking Services:

- Cyprus boasts a sophisticated banking infrastructure, with many ATMs (Automated Teller Machines) easily accessible in towns, cities, and well-liked tourist locations. Withdrawing cash from an ATM is convenient because most major foreign credit and debit cards are accepted by them. When using your card in Cyprus, be sure to inquire about any potential foreign transaction fees with your bank.

Currency Exchange:
- Banks and exchange offices, often known as exchange bureaus, are located in most major cities if you need to convert foreign currency into euros. Furthermore, a lot of hotels offer currency exchange services; nevertheless, their conversion rates may not be as good as those offered by banks.

Credit Cards:
- In Cyprus, credit cards are extensively accepted, particularly Visa and Mastercard. A credit card can be used for the majority of purchases, including travel, dining, and retail. Carrying cash, though, is a smart idea at markets, smaller establishments, and other locations that might not take credit or debit cards.

Banking Hours:

- In Cyprus, the standard banking hours are 8:30 AM to 1:30 PM, Monday through Friday. In larger cities or popular tourist destinations, certain branches might provide Saturday services or longer hours. ATMs are open around the clock for cash withdrawals.

Traveler's checks:
- Since credit cards and ATMs are so widely used, traveler's checks are becoming less prevalent. For convenience, it's best to rely on these more contemporary payment methods.

To make sure you can use your cards without any problems, let your bank know about your vacation intentions before you go. Furthermore, find out about any foreign transaction costs related to your banking services as well as the current currency rates. Having local cash on hand, familiarity with the banking system, and awareness of your preferred payment options will make handling money during your travel to Cyprus around the clock.

Chapter 3

Traveling to Cyprus

Due to its well-connected transportation system, traveling to Cyprus is not too difficult. Both Larnaca International Airport and Paphos International Airport, which serve tourists from all over the world, are located in Cyprus. You may easily locate accessible air travel options to make your trip to Cyprus effortless, regardless of your origin—Europe, the Middle East, or other regions of the globe.

Aircraft and Airports

Cyprus has two sizable international airports that act as entry points to the island:

1. Larnaca International Airport (LCA):
- The biggest and busiest airport in Cyprus is situated on the southeast coast. It has excellent connections to many locations in Europe, the

Middle East, and other regions. Modern amenities available at the airport include restaurants, duty-free stores, automobile rental services, and ways to get around the island.

2. **Paphos International Airport (PFO):**
- The second-largest airport in Cyprus, Paphos Airport is located on the western coast. It is a well-liked starting point for tourists looking to explore the island's western attractions because it mainly services charter and low-cost carriers. Numerous airlines provide flights to and from Cyprus, giving visitors many options. Aegean Airlines, British Airways, Ryanair, Cyprus Airways, and many more are notable airlines. It's important to verify with your preferred airline and book your flights well in advance, especially during busy travel times, as flight availability and itineraries may vary seasonally. When you arrive at the airport in Larnaca or Paphos, the immigration and customs processes operate smoothly.

To bring you to your final destination, both airports provide easy transit alternatives such as buses, taxis, and rental cars. Before your journey, it is advisable to check flight times, purchase your tickets, and arrange for your transportation from the airport to your lodging. Cyprus offers visitors from all over the world a warm and practical entrance point with its well-connected airports and a range of airlines.

Points of Entry

Cyprus entry ports:

Cyprus provides several entrance ports that enable visitors to reach the island by water in addition to its international airports. These ports of entry serve a variety of patrons, including cruise passengers and tourists. An overview of Cyprus's main entry ports is provided below:

1. Limassol Port:

- The primary seaport of Cyprus is situated in Limassol, which is on the southern coast of the island. It is a frequent destination for cruise ships and plays a significant part in Cyprus's trade and commerce. When arriving at Limassol Port, visitors can take in the lively atmosphere, interesting historical buildings, and stunning beaches of the city. The port provides quick access to neighboring attractions as well as the city heart of Limassol.

2. Larnaca Port:

- In addition to housing one of Cyprus's international airports, Larnaca is home to a marina and a passenger terminal for ferries and cruise ships. The eastern portion of the island, including Larnaca itself and neighboring places like Ayia Napa and Protaras, is easily accessible from this entry point.

3. **Paphos Port:**
   - Paphos, a city on the western coast, has a tiny harbor that can hold boats and cruise ships. After arriving at Paphos Port, visitors can enjoy the archeological sites and tour the old city. They can also visit other well-liked locations in the area, like the Troodos Mountains and the Akamas Peninsula.

4. **Famagusta Port:**
   - Situated inside the Turkish Republic of Northern Cyprus, Famagusta Port is situated in the country's northern region. Because a different government controls the northern section of the island, access through this port requires distinct visa and entry procedures. When using this port, visitors should be mindful of the political climate and adhere to the relevant entrance requirements.

The entry ports of Cyprus provide a kind greeting and easy access to all areas of the island, whether you are traveling there by boat or for other nautical pursuits. It is important to verify the prerequisites for entry, the processes for customs, and any other laws that apply to your particular mode of entry and the activities you want to undertake while visiting Cyprus.

Chapter 4

Recommendations

Let's have a look at our lodging alternatives as we get ready for our journey in Cyprus. There is much to discover, from quaint resorts to villas by the sea. Your choices and thoughts? I'm eager to look into lodging choices as we organize our trip to Cyprus. There's much to pick from, including quaint cottages and beachside resorts. Together, let's explore our tastes and make the most of our time here on this stunning island!

Resorts and Hotels

A wide variety of hotels and resorts in Cyprus are available to suit different tastes and price ranges. A sneak peek at what to expect is as follows:

1. Coastal Resorts:

- Cyprus offers an abundance of opulent coastal resorts for visitors looking for a beachside paradise. These provide amenities including private beaches, spas, and water sports in addition to breathtaking views of the Mediterranean.

2. enchanting Villas:
- Cyprus is renowned for its enchanting villas tucked away in scenic villages. For those who want to fully immerse themselves in the local way of life, renting a villa offers a distinctive and genuine experience.

3. Boutique Hotels:
- The island is home to a variety of boutique hotels, many of which are located in chic modern or historic buildings. These hotels provide individualized care along with a dash of sophistication.

4. More Affordable Options:
- Cyprus offers a range of guesthouses and small hotels that offer cozy stays without going over the price for those on a tighter budget.

5. **Conventional Agrotourism:**
  - You might look at agrotourism possibilities for a more immersive trip. These entail visiting rural farms and living like a native Cypriot.

You can find solutions that suit different hobbies and tastes in addition to these types of accommodations. To help us narrow down our options, kindly let me know your preferences and any unique needs you may have. Choosing the ideal lodging can significantly improve our experience in Cyprus, a stunning location with a lot to offer. I'm excited to talk about this in more detail and make this vacation one to remember.

Low-Cost Lodging

Cyprus, which is well-known for its breathtaking scenery and friendly people, also has a variety of affordable lodging options that let you explore the island without going over budget. This is what to anticipate:

1. Guesthouses and Inns:
  - Convenient and reasonably priced lodging is provided by small guesthouses and inns. These

family-run businesses frequently offer a personal touch and cultural insights. If you want a cozy but reasonably-priced experience, this is a great choice.

2. Apartment Rentals:

- If you're going on a group trip, renting an apartment for self-catering may be a more economical option. By choosing this option, you can cook for yourself and cut down on eating out costs.

3. Camping and Caravan Sites:

- Cyprus has stunning natural surroundings for camping and caravan sites, perfect for outdoor enthusiasts. Although it calls for a more daring mindset, this is a reasonably priced opportunity to take in the island's unspoiled scenery.

4. Low-Cost Hotels:

- There are also several inexpensive hotels in Cyprus. These may not have the amenities of upscale resorts, but they can offer a cozy and practical starting point for island exploration.

These low-cost lodging options allow you to maximize your Cyprus vacation without sacrificing the experience. Once I have your preferences, travel dates, and any special needs, we can look into finding the best low-cost lodging choices for our journey.

Outdoor and Camping Provisions

Cyprus is a haven for outdoor enthusiasts, offering a plethora of chances for those seeking outdoor adventures. An outline of a few of the choices is provided below:

1. Campsites:
- There are many clean, well-maintained camping areas in Cyprus. These are frequently located in beautiful natural environments, such as coastal or alpine regions. Camping is a great opportunity to take in the stunning scenery of the island and spend starry nights. Numerous campgrounds

provide modest amenities and a true sensation of being outside.

2. **Hiking and Trekking:**
   - There are numerous hiking trails on the island, some leading to craggy mountain summits and others passing through verdant forests. Some pathways are appropriate for hikers of all skill levels, whether they are novices or experts. The trekking prospects in the Troodos Mountains are very well-known.

3. **Water Sports:**
   - Cyprus is a haven for lovers of water sports because of its pristine waters. You can enjoy sports like sailing, windsurfing, scuba diving, and snorkeling. The island's shoreline offers a wealth of opportunities to discover undersea marvels.

4. **Jeep Safaris and Off-Roading:**
   - If you're looking for an exciting experience, think about going on a Jeep Safari or an off-roading adventure. These trips offer you a sense of the island's more secluded and pristine regions as they take you across challenging terrain.

5. Bird Watching:

- For migratory birds, Cyprus is an important stopover. Ornithologists and nature lovers will find great chances for bird watching in the Akrotiri Salt Lake and other wetlands.

6. Rock Climbing:

- Rock climbers of all skill levels can enjoy the rugged terrain and limestone cliffs found across Cyprus.

Our outdoor activities can be customized to fit your skill level and interests. An adventure awaits you, whether it's camping beneath the starry Cyprus sky, hiking through the Troodos Mountains, or submerging yourself in the undersea realm.

Chapter 5

Regions and Cities of Cyprus

There are many different areas and cities to discover on the stunning and diverse island of Cyprus. Every location offers a different experience, from Limassol's charming coastline setting to Nicosia's busy streets.

Greece

The capital of Cyprus, Nicosia, is a diverse and historically significant city. With the Green Line acting as a buffer between the northern Turkish Cypriot and southern Greek Cypriot sides, it is split into two distinct halves. The complicated history of the island led to this partition, making Nicosia the last divided capital city globally. The current face of Nicosia may be found in the southern part of the city, where there are bustling streets, modern shops and restaurants, and a dynamic environment. The city's rich history is showcased by its old center, which is surrounded by Venetian walls and contains historic sites including the Cyprus Museum and the St. Sophia Cathedral (now Selimiye Mosque).

You enter a new world with distinctly Turkish Cypriot architecture, food, and culture when you cross the Green Line into the northern section of Nicosia. Notable landmarks include the centuries-old caravanserai known as the Buyuk Han and the Selimiye Mosque. Following are some salient points:

1. History and Culture:

- Discover the city's historical core inside Old Nicosia's Venetian walls. See the Leventis Municipal Museum to have a better understanding of the history of the city, and the Cyprus Museum to learn about the rich archeological legacy of the island.

2. Ledra Street:

- Take a stroll down Ledra Street, a busy commercial and dining area that crosses the city's Green Line. You can switch between the Turkish and Greek Cypriot teams here.

3. Selimiye Mosque (previously St. Sophia church):
- This mosque, which was formerly a Gothic church constructed in the thirteenth century, is a sight to behold. It is a representation of the city's intricate past.

4. Green Line:
- Nicosia is the world's final divided capital, with a buffer zone under UN supervision dividing the two sides. To gain an understanding of the current political climate, you can visit the buffer zone.

5. Modern Nicosia:
- With its cutting-edge eateries, boutiques, and cultural institutions, the southern portion of the city is a bustling modern metropolis. The city offers a diverse range of cultures in a vibrant environment.

6. Local Cuisine:
- Treat yourself to authentic Cypriot fare at neighborhood tavernas, and don't forget to sample some Turkish Cypriot delicacies up in the north.

Nicosia is a unique and intriguing tourist destination since it is a city where history and modern life mix. Discover its rich history, stroll through its varied neighborhoods, and take in the friendly warmth of its residents. A spot where history and contemporary life meet, Nicosia's division serves as a reminder of the current political climate in Cyprus. Discover the contrasts, stroll about the city's two sides, and learn about the intricate history of the island. A fascinating and enlightening voyage through time and culture may be found in Nicosia.

Limassol

The second-biggest city in Cyprus, Limassol, also known as Lemesos, is located on the island's southern coast. This thriving seaside city is well-known for its lively atmosphere, extensive history, and an array of tourist and local-friendly attractions.

Crucial Pointers:

1. Beaches and Waterfront:
- Limassol has an exquisite coastline that includes lovely beaches. The beaches, such as Dasoudi Beach and Lady's Mile Beach, offer chances for water sports and sunbathing, while the city's lengthy promenade is ideal for strolls.

2. Historic Old Town:
- Take a tour of Limassol's quaint old town, which features cobblestone lanes, typical Cypriot architecture, and old structures like Limassol Castle, which houses the Medieval Museum.

3. Dining and Wine:
- The city of Limassol is well known for its wine culture. Enjoy the opportunity to explore nearby wineries and sample some of the island's best wines. With a large number of eateries serving both foreign and Cypriot cuisine, the city also boasts a varied culinary scene.

4. Festivals and Events:
- All year long, Limassol is home to several festivals and events. Popular events include the

Limassol Beer Festival, Wine Festival, and Carnival.

5. Nightlife:
- The city has a thriving nightlife culture that makes it come to life at night. Bars, clubs, and venues along the shore are open late into the morning.

6. Modern Developments:
- Limassol has grown significantly in the last several years, and its cosmopolitan appeal is enhanced by luxury hotels, modern developments, and a marina.

7. Cultural Experiences:
- Take in the history of the island by visiting the Limassol Archaeological Museum and exploring the Municipal Gardens, a peaceful area right in the middle of the city.

8. Access and Location:
- Limassol is easily accessible from both the Larnaca and Paphos International Airports due to its handy southern coast location. The city has good road connectivity to other areas of Cyprus.

9. **Local customs:**
- With a blend of Mediterranean and Greek influences, Limassol, like the rest of Cyprus, has a rich cultural past. The city's distinct character is enhanced by the celebration of customs and traditional events.

Limassol has plenty to offer visitors, whether they want to explore historical monuments, unwind on the beach, or take advantage of the vibrant nightlife. The city is vibrant, showcasing Cyprus's contemporary side while acknowledging its rich historical past.

The Paphos

Situated on Cyprus's southwest coast, Paphos is a city rich in mythology, history, and scenic beauty. Travelers looking for a combination of culture and relaxation love this enchanted location because of its breathtaking coastline, abundant archaeological monuments, and laid-back Mediterranean atmosphere.

Important Points to Note:

1. **Archaeological Marvels:**
   - Paphos is home to numerous archaeological monuments, many of which are included in the UNESCO World Heritage List. Of them, the Tombs of the Kings, a collection of prehistoric burial chambers, and the Odeon amphitheater, with its elaborate mosaics, are the highlights of the Paphos Archaeological Park.

2. **Mythological Significance:**
   - The Greek goddess of love and beauty Aphrodite is said to have been born in Paphos. You can tour Aphrodite's Rock and pay a visit to Petra tou Romiou, the mythological birthplace of Aphrodite.

3. **Beaches & Scenic Coastline:**
   - Paphos has a range of beaches, from quiet coves to shorelines ideal for families. Popular spots for swimming and water sports are Coral Bay and Lara Beach.

4. **Old Town Charm:**
   - Take a tour of Paphos's quaint Old Town, which features vibrant buildings, traditional

architecture, and active marketplaces. There's also a charming historic port in the city center where you may have dinner by the water.

5. Akamas Peninsula:
- Hikers and lovers of the outdoors will find paradise in the neighboring Akamas Peninsula. Its untamed landscapes, canyons, and seaside pathways provide amazing vistas and chances for outdoor exploration.

6. Culinary Delights:
- Paphos has a thriving restaurant scene with both international and traditional Cypriot fare. Make sure to sample some of the regional specialties, such as fresh seafood and grilled halloumi cheese.

7. Cultural Experiences:
- Throughout the year, the city holds several festivals and cultural events, including plays, concerts, and exhibitions of artwork. Opera fans should not miss the Paphos Aphrodite Festival.

8. **Accessibility:**
- Travelers may readily reach Paphos thanks to its international airport. The city has good road access to various areas of Cyprus.

Paphos has a singular fusion of natural beauty, mythology, and history. Paphos offers a variety of travel experiences, including touring historic ruins, unwinding on the beach, and learning about the island's rich cultural history. This location offers the allure of antiquated legend combined with contemporary amenities and breathtaking scenery.

Les Arcs

The attractive city of Larnaca, which is situated on Cyprus' southern coast, is well-known for its stunning beaches, intriguing past, and hospitable Mediterranean vibe. Travelers looking for a combination of leisure and cultural exploration frequently choose to visit this coastal jewel.

Crucial Pointers:

1. **Finikoudes Beach:**
    - One of Larnaca's most well-known tourist attractions is Finikoudes Beach. Its golden dunes, crystal-clear blue waters, and promenade bordered with palm trees make it the ideal place for swimming and tanning.
2. **St. Lazarus Church:**
    - Take a tour of this magnificent example of Byzantine architecture, which dates back centuries. The saint Lazarus, whose tomb is thought to be in Larnaca, is honored by the church's name.
3. **Hala Sultan Tekke:**
    - Take a trip to the tranquil salt flats that encircle the revered Muslim mausoleum. For Muslims, this magnificent location is a major pilgrimage site.
4. **Larnaca Salt Lake:**
    - During the winter, flamingo flocks can be found in this city's well-known salt lake. It's a special place with a lovely backdrop to go birdwatching.
5. **Kamares Aqueduct:**

- A historic landmark that highlights the city's cultural legacy, the Kamares Aqueduct is an Ottoman engineering masterpiece.

6. **Museums:**
   - Learn more about the history and artistic expression of the island at Larnaca's many museums, which include the Pierides Museum and the Larnaca Archaeological Museum.

7. **Culinary Delights:**
   - Sample traditional delicacies like souvlaki, moussaka, and loukoumades at neighborhood tavernas and restaurants. Savor the flavors of Cyprus cuisine.

8. **Accessibility:**
   - As a main entry point into the city, Larnaca International Airport offers travelers ease. The city has good road connectivity to other areas of Cyprus.

A beautiful fusion of natural beauty and history may be found in the city of Larnaca. Larnaca has something for every type of traveler, whether they wish to explore historic monuments, unwind on the beach, or become fully immersed in the local way of life.

Augustina

The city of Famagusta, also called Gazimağusa in Turkish, is situated on Cyprus's eastern coast. With its unique blend of ancient and modern influences, rich cultural legacy, and unique position in the island's history, this city is special.

Principal Aspects:

1. Historic Walled City:
- The well-preserved medieval walls that enclose Famagusta are its most recognizable feature. Constructed in the era of Lusignan, these walls provide witness to the city's former prominence as a commercial and strategic center.

2. Othello' Tower:
- The famous castle inside the walled city known as Othello's Tower is frequently associated with William Shakespeare's play "Othello." In addition to offering expansive views of the surroundings,

the tower gives an insight into the colorful past of Famagusta.

3. **St. Nicholas Cathedral:**
   - Located inside the old town are the ruins of St. Nicholas Cathedral, a magnificent 14th-century Gothic architectural specimen.

4. **Golden Beaches:**
   - Glapsides Beach and Palm Beach, two of Famagusta's stunning sandy beaches, are well-known. Beach enthusiasts will find the Mediterranean Sea's gorgeous seas to be their ideal destination.

5. **Varosha:**
   - Known for its turbulent past, Varosha is a district in Famagusta. It was formerly a bustling tourist destination, but since Turkey invaded Cyprus in 1974, it has remained abandoned.

6. **Salamis Ruins:**
   - The ancient city of Salamis, which was founded in the eleventh century BC, can be explored. It is located just north of Famagusta. Roman baths, a theater, and a gymnasium are among the

well-preserved structures found at the archaeological site.

7. Cultural Diversity:
- With traces of Greek, Turkish, and Venetian ancestry, Famagusta is a reflection of the many cultural influences that have influenced Cyprus throughout the ages.

8. Accessibility:
- The Turkish Republic of Northern Cyprus (TRNC) is home to Famagusta. Ercan International Airport is the primary entry point for foreign visitors to the area and provides access to the city.

A live example of Cyprus's rich cultural diversity and history is Famagusta. It is a remarkable city of contrasts, with its gorgeous beaches, medieval fortifications, and ancient ruins.

Mountains of Troodos

The majestic and untamed Troodos Mountains span much of the central portion of the island, and they are situated in the center of Cyprus. Rich cultural and historical significance, picturesque mountain communities, and verdant landscapes are the hallmarks of this remarkable natural wonder.

Principal Aspects:

1. Natural Beauty:
- For those who love the outdoors, the Troodos Mountains are a haven. Dense forests, charming valleys, and a wide variety of plants and animals define the area. Hikers, outdoor enthusiasts, and nature lovers all flock to this well-liked location.

2. Hiking paths:
- There is a network of hiking paths in the Troodos Mountains that are suitable for both novice and expert hikers. These paths lead to tranquil monasteries, tumbling waterfalls, and beautiful vistas.

3. Traditional Villages:

- You may enjoy the warmth and culture of the locals in the traditional Cypriot villages scattered throughout the mountain range. Explore quaint villages such as Platres, Omodos, and Kakopetria.

4. **Byzantine Churches:**
   - Several Byzantine churches and monasteries, several of which are UNESCO World Heritage Sites, may be found in the Troodos Mountains. The beautiful paintings that cover the painted churches in the area serve as a tribute to Cyprus's rich cultural legacy.

5. **Winter Sports:**
   - The Troodos Mountains become a popular site for winter sports during the winter. There are ski and snowboarding chances at the Mount Olympus Ski Resort.

6. **Troodos Geopark:**
   - This location is acknowledged for its significance in terms of geology. Learn about the

geological past of the island by visiting places with lava flows and mineral deposits.

7. **Troodos Wineries:**
   - The area is renowned for having wineries and vineyards. Don't pass up the opportunity to sample the regional wines, which are renowned for having distinctive characteristics.

8. **Accessible Location:**
   - The Troodos Mountains are a well-liked day trip or weekend escape destination for both locals and visitors since they are conveniently accessible from large towns like Limassol and Nicosia.

Cyprus's coastal regions can be refreshed by visiting the Troodos Mountains. Indulging in historical and cultural exploration, taking in the serene atmosphere of the mountainsSeveralavoring the pure beauty of nature—the Troodos Mountains provide something for everyone who comes. You can learn about the island's rich history and establish a connection with nature there.

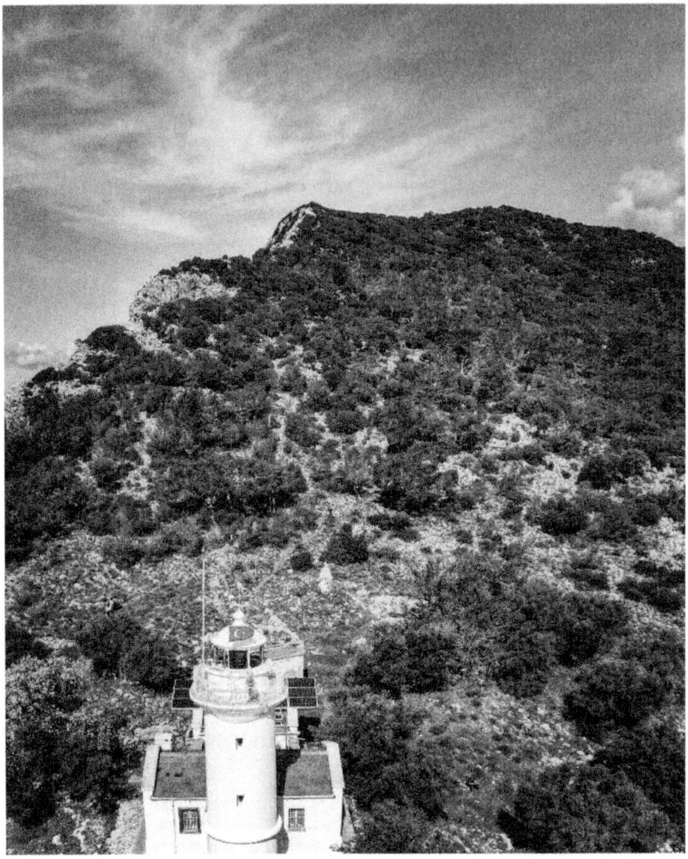

Chapter 6

Leading Attractions and Monuments

Explore Cyprus's most popular sites and landmarks to learn about the country's rich history and stunning scenery. Discover historic sites like the Tombs of the Kings and Paphos Archaeological Park, unwind on gorgeous beaches like Nissi Beach, take a stroll through the breathtaking Troodos Mountains, and learn about the past at St. Lazarus Church and the medieval walls of Famagusta. As you take in this alluring island's Mediterranean beauty, don't forget to enjoy the regional food and wine."

Archaeological Sites and Ancient Ruins

Cyprus offers an intriguing tour through its rich history and the civilizations that have left their imprint on the island. The island is home to a plethora of historical ruins and archeological monuments. These locations demonstrate the island's cultural significance and offer a glimpse into its past.

Important Websites

1. Paphos Archaeological Park:
- This expansive complex in Paphos, home to the Odeon amphitheater, ancient theaters, and Roman villas with elaborate mosaics, is a UNESCO World Heritage site. It is evidence of the Roman ancestry of the island.

2. Tombs of the Kings:
- This Hellenistic-era necropolis, which is close to Paphos, has underground tombs and rooms cut out of the rock. These magnificent tombs provide

insight into the burial customs of prehistoric Cyprus.

3. **Salamis:**
   - This ancient city, which dates to the eleventh century BC, is located in the Famagusta district. Discover the well-preserved Roman baths, theater, and gymnasium remains.

4. **Kourion:**
   - This historic city is a reminder of the island's classical heritage, with its Greco-Roman theater overlooking the sea. It's a breathtaking southern shore archaeological site.

5. **Choirokoitia:**
   - A UNESCO World Heritage site, this Neolithic settlement provides a rare chance to discover prehistoric Cyprus. The remarkably preserved round homes and artifacts shed light on prehistoric human society.

6. **Amathus:**
   - Originally a significant ancient city, Amathus is situated close to Limassol. The Phoenician and

Greek influences on the island can be seen in the ruins, which include a regal acropolis and an agora.

7. old Idalion:
- Idalion is an archaeological site that is located close to Dali today. Its temples, fortifications, and tombs provide insight into the past of the old city.

8. Kalavasos-Tenta:
- With its well-preserved structures and artifacts, this Chalcolithic settlement provides insights into Cyprus's Copper Age.

In addition to offering a window into Cyprus's past, these ancient ruins and archaeological sites advance our knowledge of the history of the wider Mediterranean region. For history buffs and anybody curious about the island's cultural legacy, they are a must-see.

Water Sports and Beaches

Cyprus is well known for having some of the most exquisite beaches in the Mediterranean along its stunning coastline. The island provides a variety of beach and water-related activities, whether you're looking for undersea adventures, thrilling water sports, or just relaxing on golden sands.

Principal Aspects:

1. Golden Beaches:
- There is a beach in Cyprus to suit every taste, from the energetic Finikoudes Beach in Larnaca to the tranquil beauty of Fig Tree Bay in Protaras. Soft sands and crystal-clear waves make for the ideal beachcombing and sunbathing environment.

2. Water Sports:
- Cyprus has plenty to offer adventure seekers. At several coastal hotspots, such as Nissi Beach in Ayia Napa, try your hand at water sports like windsurfing, jet skiing, parasailing, and scuba diving.

3. Aphrodite's Rock:
- See the fabled Aphrodite's Rock (Petra tou Romiou), where the goddess of love is said to have been born. With its famous sea stack and glistening clean waters, it provides a lovely backdrop for a romantic dip.

4. Boat rides:
- Take boat rides to see the coast from an alternative viewpoint. From different coastal villages, you can go on leisurely cruises, adventures with a pirate theme, and even fishing trips.

5. Kitesurfing in Limassol:
- Because of its consistent winds and ideal conditions, Limassol is a popular destination for kitesurfers. There are kitesurfing programs and rental choices available for all skill levels.

6. Kayaking and Stand-Up Paddleboarding:
- While kayaking or paddleboarding along the shore, discover undiscovered coves and serene bays. There are very picturesque trails on the Akamas Peninsula.

7. Beach Bars and Restaurants:
- There are several beach bars and restaurants along the coast where you may enjoy Cypriot food, cool cocktails, and waterfront views.

Beachcombers, thrill seekers, and water enthusiasts can enjoy a variety of experiences on Cyprus's beaches and water sports. The island's coastline attractions, whether you're surfing waves, plunging into the ocean, or just enjoying the sun, will undoubtedly leave you with unforgettable experiences.

Cultural Centers and Museums

Cyprus is a historical and culturally rich country with a wide variety of museums and cultural institutions that offer windows into the island's rich past. These museums display everything from ancient antiquities to modern artwork, providing visitors with an insightful trip through time.

Principal Aspects:

1. **Cyprus Museum (Nicosia):**
   - Housed in the nation's capital, Nicosia, the Cyprus Museum boasts an extensive collection of artifacts ranging from prehistoric times to the Roman Empire. Its displays illuminate Cyprus's

rich history through sculptures, ceramics, and jewelry.

2. Limassol Archaeological Museum:
- This museum uses Neolithic relics, tools, and ceramics to provide light on the history of Limassol and the surrounding area.

3. Byzantine Museum and Art Galleries (Nicosia):
- This museum, which is situated in Nicosia, features frescoes from churches and monasteries, religious objects, and icons.

4. Pierides Museum (Larnaca):
- The Pierides Museum in Larnaca is renowned for its remarkable collection of antiques from Cyprus, which includes artifacts from many eras.

5. Leventis Municipal Museum of Nicosia:
- Specializing in the history of the city, these perspectives, images, and records show how the capital has changed over time.

6. Cyprus Classic Motorcycle Museum (Larnaca):
- This museum offers a distinct cultural perspective and showcases a rare collection of classic motorcycles for motorcycle aficionados.

7. **The Cyprus Wine Museum (Erimi, Limassol):**
   - This museum showcases the island's longstanding connection to viticulture and offers an exploration of the history of Cypriot winemaking.

8. **Bank of Cyprus Cultural Foundation (Nicosia):**
   - Through events, exhibitions, and a comprehensive archive of manuscripts and papers, this cultural hub promotes Cypriot art and culture.

One can gain a deeper understanding of Cyprus's legacy, from its ancient times to modern artistic expressions, by visiting these museums and cultural institutes. The cultural institutions of Cyprus are a great place to visit if you're interested in learning more about the island's rich and varied past, regardless of your interests in religious art, modern culture, or ancient civilizations.

Natural Attractions and Parks

Cyprus provides a wealth of parks and natural beauties for those who enjoy the outdoors thanks to its varied landscapes and Mediterranean climate. The island's natural beauty, which includes tranquil marshes and lush forests, is a haven for anyone looking for outdoor activities and peaceful settings.

Crucial Pointers:

1. Troodos Mountains:
- Nestled in the center of Cyprus, the Troodos Mountains are a breathtaking natural marvel, including verdant valleys, hiking trails, and thick forests. Hikers, nature enthusiasts, and those who enjoy peaceful mountain scenery can find paradise in this area.

2. Akamas Peninsula:
- Located in the island's northwest, this unspoiled wilderness area features canyons, steep inclines, and an abundance of luxuriant vegetation. Hiking, boat rides, and vehicle safaris are all highly recommended in this area.

3. Akamas Blue Lagoon:

- For swimmers and snorkelers, the pristine waters of Akamas Blue Lagoon are an oasis. Surrounded by stunning rocks, the lagoon's dazzling blue waters.

4. Troodos Geopark:
- A UNESCO Global Geopark recognized for its distinctive geological structures, like as lava flows and mineral deposits, this park is a geological wonder.

5. The Akrotiri Salt Lake:
- Situated close to Larnaca, this important wetland habitat is home to flamingos and other wintering bird species. It's a well-liked location for bird watching.

Discovering the parks and natural wonders of Cyprus offers an opportunity to re-establish a connection with nature and to recognize the island's distinctive biodiversity. These natural wonders, which range from idyllic seaside settings to mountainous terrain, present chances for exploration, leisure, and admiration of the remarkable natural legacy of the island.

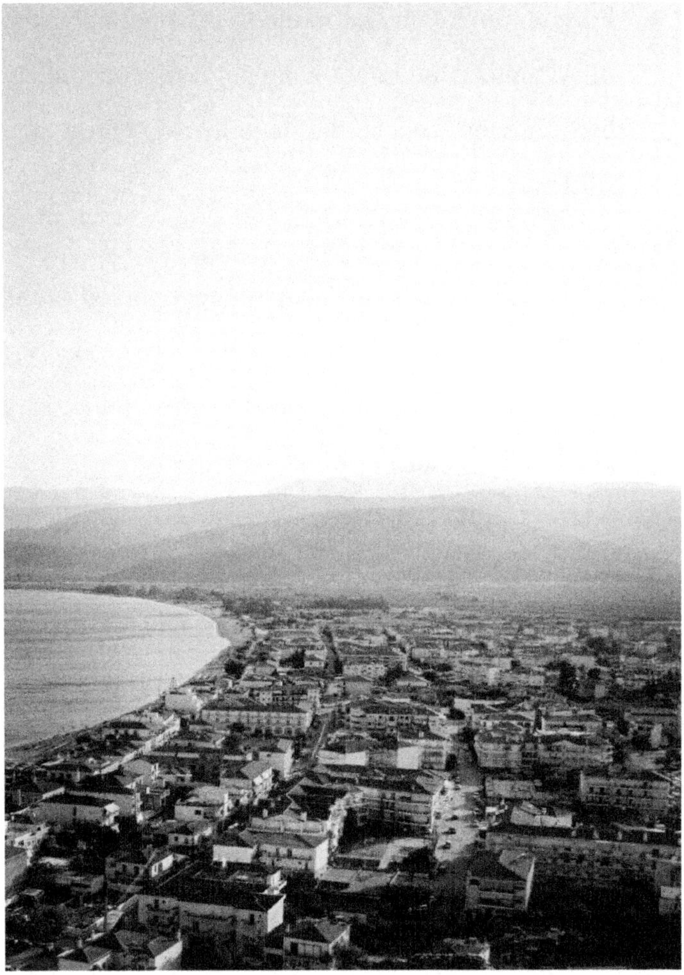

Chapter 7

Sports and Entertainment

"With a variety of entertainment options, take in Cyprus's lively pulse. The island provides countless opportunities to create lifelong experiences, from exciting beach parties in Ayia Napa to discovering historic ruins, relishing Cypriot cuisine, and engaging in water sports. Cyprus offers something for everyone to enjoy, regardless of your interests—culture, sun, or adventure."

Exploration of Nature and Hiking

Hikers and lovers of the great outdoors will find nirvana in Cyprus with its varied landscapes and breathtaking views. The island is a great place for people looking for outdoor adventure and a close connection to nature because it has a variety of hiking paths that wind through verdant forests, striking mountains, and coastal cliffs.

Principal Aspects:

1. Caledonia Waterfalls:
- The Caledonia Waterfalls provide a wonderful trekking experience, tucked away in a shaded, calm ravine in the Troodos Mountains.

2. Cape Greco National Forest Park:
- Located at the southeast point of the island, Cape Greco has rugged cliffs, sea caves, and magnificent coastal walks. Hiking and trekking in the distinctive scenery of the area are highly recommended in the Cape Greco National Forest Park.

3. Avakas Gorge:
- This remarkable gorge, which is close to Akamas, has cliffs and tight spaces. A hike through Avakas Gorge is a once-in-a-lifetime experience.

4. Machairas Forest:

- This forest is well-known for its hiking trails and religious significance. After passing through this woodland, one arrives at the peaceful Monastery of Machairas.

5. **Cedar Valley in Paphos Forest:**
    - This tranquil region of Paphos Forest is renowned for its centuries-old cedar trees. The forest is a popular hiking location and offers a refreshing respite in the summer.

6. **Troodos Botanical Garden:**
    - With a wide variety of local plants to explore, this garden, which is nestled in the Troodos Mountains, is a haven for nature enthusiasts.

In Cyprus, hiking and nature exploration provide a singular experience of being fully immersed in the unspoiled natural environment of the island. The paths offer opportunities to observe the beauty of Cyprus's varied landscapes at varying degrees of effort.

After Dark and Entertainment

With a thriving nightlife and entertainment scene, Cyprus understands how to make the night last. For those looking to dance the night away, take in live music, or sample Cypriot cuisine outside beneath the stars, the island provides a variety of alternatives, from vibrant coastal cities to quaint village tavernas.

Crucial Pointers:

1. Beach Parties in Ayia Napa:
- The lively beach parties and exciting nightlife culture in Ayia Napa are well known. This seaside town is a nightlife attraction with its beach bars, outdoor stages, and international DJs.

2. Limassol's Nightclubs:
- An active nightlife can be found in Limassol, the cosmopolitan center of Cyprus. Partygoers of all stripes are catered to by the city's clubs, taverns, and live music venues.

3. Larnaca Waterfront:
- At night, the charming waterfront of Larnaca comes alive with a plethora of eateries, clubs, and bars that offer stunning views of the sea. In a laid-back atmosphere, take in drinks and live music.

4. Traditional Tavernas:

- Cyprus's traditional tavernas and village celebrations are well-known, even outside of the coastal cities. With regional cuisine, music, and dancing, these quaint places provide a genuine cultural experience.

5. **Old Town in Nicosia:**
   - Old Town in Nicosia is home to a variety of hip cafés, bars, and art galleries. The city's nightlife culture blends contemporary entertainment with a backdrop of history.

6. **Music and performances:**
   - All year long, Cyprus is home to several music festivals and performances. Savor a variety of musical styles, ranging from jazz and rock to traditional Cypriot tunes.

7. **Casino Nights:**
   - Several casinos in Cyprus provide gaming, shows, and live entertainment. Play the slots and gaming tables to see how lucky you are.

8. **Dinner and Shows:**
   - Dinner and entertainment packages with live music, dancing performances, and theatrical

productions are available at numerous restaurants throughout the island.

Whether you want calm evenings in a beautiful environment, partying all night, or both, Cyprus's nightlife and entertainment have something to offer everyone. With so many things to choose from, the island offers a vibrant setting for making special nights and soaking in the warmth of Cypriot hospitality. Cyprus has a colorful nightlife where you may party, eat, and dance long into the Mediterranean night.

Markets and shopping

A lovely shopping experience combining historic markets and contemporary retail therapy can be found in Cyprus. The island offers a wide range of shopping options to suit every taste, whether you're looking for high-end labels, regional handicrafts, or fresh fruit.

Crucial Pointers:
1.Shop at Boutiques:
- The seaside towns of Nicosia, Limassol, and Larnaca are well-known for their high-end

boutiques and global designer retailers. You can purchase jewelry, accessories, and high-end clothing.

2. **Traditional Markets:**
   - The "agoras," or traditional markets of Cyprus, are vivacious. The Municipal Market in Paphos and the Laiki Geitonia in Nicosia are great places to browse for locally made goods and get a taste of Cypriot culture.

3. **Souvenirs and Handmade Crafts:**
   - There are a lot of locally manufactured souvenirs and crafts in Cyprus. Seek out regional lacework, linens, and ceramics in addition to customary goods like "loukoumi" (a Cypriot delicacy) and "Zivania" (a native spirit).

4. **Street Markets:**
   - Fresh vegetables, apparel, and household products are all sold by sellers in Cyprus's street markets. A window into daily life in Cyprus is provided by these markets.

5. **Farmers' Markets:**

- Take in the colorful farmers' markets where you may get locally sourced items such as dairy products, fresh produce, and fruits.

6. Shopping Alleys in Nicosia:

- Ledra and Makarios Avenue in Nicosia are per stroll around the city's trendy stores, eateries, and cafes.

7. Craft Villages:

- See craftsmen making beautiful silver jewelry and lacework at craft villages like Lefkara. The traditional craftsmanship of these settlements is well-known.

8. Ancient Bazaars:

- Discover the storied ancient bazaars of Cyprus, like the Omodos Village Square and the Buyuk Han in Nicosia, which are brimming with quaint stores and rich in history.

Discovering the distinctive goods, customs, and crafts of Cyprus can be done through shopping and market visits. The island's markets and shops are great places to enjoy the Mediterranean's shopping delights and experience the warmth of Cypriot hospitality, whether you're aiming for luxury goods, local specialties, or unique souvenirs.

Chapter 8

Food and Dining

Savor the flavors of Cyprus, where eating is a pleasant Mediterranean culinary adventure. A delicious blend of regional ingredients and influences can be found in the island's culinary heritage, which ranges from fresh seafood and grilled halloumi cheese to traditional meze feasts. Dining in Cyprus is a celebration of delectable flavors and friendly service, not just a meal."

Greek Cooking

A delicious culinary voyage into the heart of the Mediterranean may be found in Cyprus cuisine. The cuisine of the island is a wonderful and savory patchwork of flavors, reflecting its rich history and natural abundance, fusing elements from Greek, Turkish, and Middle Eastern traditions.

Principal Aspects:

1. Fresh Seafood:
- Cyprus is a seafood lover's delight with its long coastline. Mouthwatering dishes are made with fresh catches such as sea bass, red mullet, and calamari, cooked with olive oil and local herbs.

2. Halloumi Cheese:
- A speciality of Cyprus, halloumi is a distinctive cheese made from sheep's milk and occasionally goat's milk. Usually grilled and garnished with mint leaves, it's a flavorful and unique starter.

3. Meze Feasts:
- Eating meze is a traditional Cypriot meal. You can enjoy a wide range of flavors in one meal with its assortment of tiny meals, which include grilled meats, kebabs, hummus, tzatziki, and dolmades.

4. Traditional meals:
- Moussaka, stifado (beef stew), kleftiko (slow-cooked lamb), and souvlaki (grilled skewers) are just a few of the traditional meals

found in Cypriot cuisine. The island's culinary legacy is reflected in these filling dishes.

5. Olive Oil and Fresh Produce:

- Sun-ripened fruits and vegetables from the island give meals a burst of color and flavor. Olive oil is a mainstay in Cypriot cookery. Taste the "loukoumi," a popular sweet dish from Cyprus that resembles Turkish pleasure.

6. Commandaria Wine:

- Cyprus is home to one of the world's oldest wine-producing regions, Commandaria Wine. The sweet dessert wine Commandaria is known around the world for both its remarkable flavor and its historical significance.

7. Coffee and Sweets:

- Enjoy sweets like galaktoboureko, baklava, and kataifi along with strong Cypriot coffee, which is a local favorite.

8. Cultural Dining:

- Indulge in the culinary customs of the island by dining at authentic tavernas, where you can also take in live music and dancing performances.

The diversity of the island's cultures and its emphasis on using fresh, locally sourced foods are reflected in Cypriot cuisine. Every item in Cyprus's cuisine, whether you're enjoying grilled halloumi, meze at a coastal taverna, or the sweetness of Cypriot desserts, is an invitation to feel the warmth and friendliness of the country's culinary scene.

Customary Recipes

Mediterranean flavors are delightfully blended together in the rich heritage of Cypriot cuisine. The distinctive cultural fusion of the island is reflected in traditional Cypriot cuisine, which draws flavors from the Middle East, Greece, and Turkey. These tried-and-true recipes provide a genuinely authentic eating experience and are a tribute to the island's culinary legacy.

Principal Traditional Foods:

1. **Moussaka:**
   - A popular meal roasted to perfection, moussaka is made of layers of eggplant, minced meat (often lamb or beef), and a creamy béchamel sauce. It's a satisfying and filling decision.
2. **Kleftiko:**
   - Marinated in herbs and spices, kleftiko is a slow-cooked lamb or goat dish baked in a clay oven. Meat that is delicious, soft, and falls off the bone is the end result.
3. **Stifado:**
   - Usually cooked with beef or rabbit, stifado is a flavorful stew. Along with tomatoes, onions, red wine, and a variety of flavorful spices, the meat is cooked slowly.
4. **Souvlaki:**
   - Served with pita bread and a choice of accompaniments like fresh veggies and tzatziki sauce, souvlaki is a well-liked street dish made with skewers of marinated, grilled beef.
5. **Dolmades:**

- Dolmades are filled grape leaves with a blend of ground beef, rice, and herbs. These little rolls are frequently offered as a meze spread or as an appetizer.

6. **Meze:**
   - Meze stands alone as a culinary adventure. It's a selection of bite-sized, tasty items that are meant to be shared and enjoyed during a leisurely meal, ranging from dips like hummus and tzatziki to kebabs, shellfish, and vegetarian alternatives.

7. **Pilaf:**
   - Known as "pilaf" in Greek, this is a typical side dish that is cooked with rice and vermicelli noodles and is frequently flavored with herbs and broth.

8. **Loukoum:**
   - A sugary dessert made with starch, sugar, and various flavorings like citrus, pistachio, or rosewater, loukoum is akin to Turkish delight.

These traditional recipes, which combine regional products with age-old cooking methods, offer a gastronomic trip into Cyprus's history and culture. Through its delicious, age-old recipes, Cypriot food allows you to experience the heart and spirit of the island, whether you're eating at a traditional taverna or cooking for yourself. This is a delectable journey into the core of Mediterranean hospitality.

Well-liked Cafes and Restaurants

Cyprus is well known for its thriving food industry in addition to its breathtaking scenery and extensive history. The island offers something for every taste, whether you're searching for cosmopolitan cuisine, quaint cafes, or traditional Cypriot cuisine. Consider these well-known eateries and cafes when you're there:

1. Nicosia's Zanettos Taverna:
- Zanettos is a family-run taverna in the center of Nicosia that serves traditional meze, souvlaki,

and moussaka—authentic Cypriot delicacies. It's a neighborhood favorite because of the welcoming ambiance and friendly service.

2. Limassol's Artima Restaurant:

- Mediterranean and Cypriot cuisine are combined in the Artima Restaurant, which is located in Limassol's old town. In a lovely location, you may savor inventive meals, grilled meats, and fresh seafood.

3. To the Traditional Kazani Tavern in Paphos:

- To Kazani, a well-liked tavern in Paphos, is well-known for its cozy atmosphere and wide selection of traditional Cypriot fare. The wonderful halloumi cheese and the robust kleftiko are not to be missed.

4. Ayia Napa's Pyxida Fish Tavern:

- In Ayia Napa, Pyxida is a must-visit if you love seafood. With a view of the sea, the eatery serves a variety of fresh seafood dishes, such as grilled fish and delectable prawns.

5. Nicosia's Paul's Coffee Roasters:

- Paul's Coffee Roasters in Nicosia is a treasure for coffee lovers. It is well-liked as a place to get a caffeine fix because they roast own beans and offer a variety of specialty coffees.

6. Larnaca's Ta Piatakia:
- In addition to coffee or tea, Ta Piatakia is a quaint cafe in Larnaca where you can enjoy delectable Cypriot delicacies like baklava and loukoumades, which are doughnuts dipped in honey.

7. Vienna Café (Limasol):
- This chic Limassol cafe is ideal for a wonderful brunch or a relaxed afternoon tea. The cuisine, which is European-inspired, features a selection of pastries and sandwiches.

8. To Paphos (Kanoni):
- An excellent option for a romantic dinner with a view is To Kanoni in Paphos. It provides a breathtaking view of the harbor and is situated atop the old Paphos Castle.

9. The Lanraca Stove:

- Larnaca's The Stove is renowned for its modern, cosmopolitan gastronomy, which includes delectable seafood and steak dishes. A welcome atmosphere is created by the helpful service and trendy decor.

10. Ayia Napa's Mezostrati Art Café:
- In Ayia Napa, Mezostrati is a distinctive art cafe offering coffee, small meals, and local art exhibitions, combining gastronomy and culture.

These are but a handful of the delicious food and coffee options Cyprus has to offer. Cyprus offers a wide range of options to fulfill your appetite, whether you're looking for traditional flavors, foreign cuisine, or a quiet cafe to relax in.

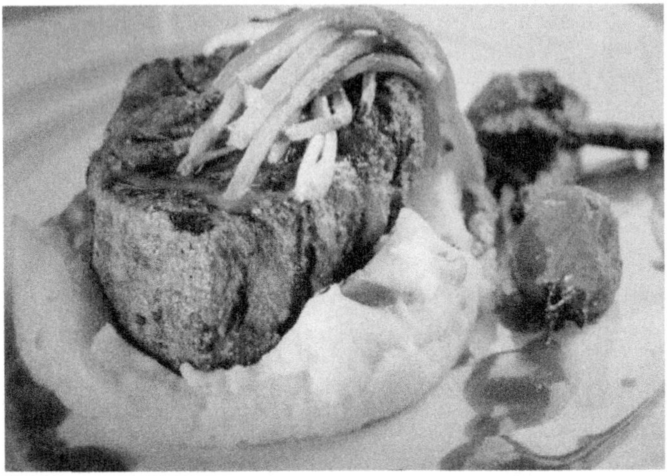

Chapter 9

Regional Events and Customs

Explore Cyprus's enthralling fusion of Turkish and Greek culinary, dance, and music traditions. Take part in the vibrant local festivals honoring customs, the arts, and delectable cuisine. Explore the cultural richness that is Cyprus.

Holidays and Religion

Cyprus is a country whose culture and legacy are greatly influenced by religion and festivals. On the island, the majority religion is Greek Orthodox; there is also a tiny Christian sect and a significant Muslim minority. An overview of Cyprus's religious landscape and annual festivals is provided here:

1. Greek Orthodox Christianity:

- Greek Orthodox Christianity is practiced by the vast majority of Cypriots. Throughout the island, there are numerous exquisitely decorated churches and monasteries, each with a unique background and purpose.

2. Religious Holidays:

- In Cyprus, Easter is arguably the most widely observed religious holiday. With candlelit processions, church services, and feasting on special Easter foods, the entire country comes to life. The Feasts of the Epiphany and the Assumption of the Virgin Mary are two more important religious holidays.

3. Multicultural Influence:

- The island of Cyprus's religious and architectural legacy have been profoundly impacted by the eras of Byzantine, Crusader, Venetian, and Ottoman dominance throughout its history. Mosques and churches can be found living in harmony together, a reflection of the island's eclectic past.

4. Muslim Holidays:

- The Turkish Cypriot population in Northern Cyprus celebrates Islamic holidays such Eid al-Fitr, Eid al-Adha, and Ramadan. These celebrations are characterized by feasts, group prayers, and a giving mood.

5. Secular Celebrations:
- Cyprus organizes a range of nonreligious festivities in addition to its religious holidays. A few examples are the Pafos Aphrodite Festival, the Larnaca Kataklysmos Water Festival, and the Limassol Carnival. These activities showcase the rich cultural heritage, history, and customs of the island.

6. Cultural Harmony:
- The cohabitation of various faiths and traditions is one of Cyprus's distinctive features. The island's ability to welcome diversity and celebrate it through a variety of festivals and activities is demonstrated by this concord between religions and cultures.

Cyprus provides a diverse range of cultural experiences, catering to both religious and secular celebrations. The island is a great place to explore and celebrate culture because there are many opportunities to immerse oneself in its history, customs, and friendly people throughout the year.

Conventional Dance and Music

Cyprus is a country whose cultural legacy is deeply rooted in music and dance. With influences from Greece, Turkey, and the Middle East, centuries of history have molded the island's traditional music and dance. A brief overview of the fascinating realm of traditional Cypriot music and dance is provided here:

1. Traditional Instruments:
- The usage of traditional instruments, such as the violin, lute, and flute, along with the bouzouki, tzouras, and baglamas (which are akin to Greek instruments), is what defines Cypriot music. Together, these instruments produce a distinctive and moving sound.

2. Traditional Cypriot Folk Music:

- Known as "Battista," traditional Cypriot folk songs frequently have lyrical topics that reflect everyday life, love, and the history of the island. Intricate musical arrangements and impassioned singing complement the songs.

3. Dancing:

- The art form of Cypriot dance is colorful and energetic. Dancers frequently move in lines or circles as they dance to the beat of traditional music. Popular dances that feature expressive motions and quick footwork include the "sousta" and "tsifteteli".

4. Regional Variations:

- Cyprus's several regions each have their own distinctive dance and music customs. For instance, the "syrtos" is a well-known dance that is performed in many different ways, with regional variations.

5. Cultural Significance:

- Weddings, religious holidays, and other significant occasions in Cyprus are not complete without traditional music and dance. These performances provide as a platform for connecting and expressing cultures.

6. **Preservation and Modern Influence:**
   - Traditional dance and music are promoted and preserved. To ensure that these antiquated artistic styles remain relevant in the modern era, many Cypriot artists incorporate modern elements into their works.

7. **Festivals and Events:**
   - Cyprus holds a number of festivals and events all year long that feature traditional dance and music. Both natives and guests can fully immerse themselves in the rich cultural legacy of the island during these meetings.

Discovering Cyprus's traditional dance and music is an enthralling trip through the core of the island's culture. It's a world of captivating songs, intense beats, and emotive motions that capture the heritage, culture, and exuberance of the Cypriot people. Cyprus provides a distinct and lively experience for everyone, regardless of preference for dancing or music.

Spoken Word and Listening

Cyprus is a fascinating historical Mediterranean island with a linguistic environment that is distinct and reflects its cosmopolitan background. To fully appreciate your vacation, it is essential to grasp the languages and communication patterns of Cyprus. This is a synopsis:

1. The Official Linguistics:
- The official languages of Cyprus are Greek and Turkish, signifying the two principal ethnic groups, Greek and Turkish Cypriots.

2. Language in Greek:
- The majority of people on the island speak Greek, especially Greek Cypriots. There are clear regional differences in the Cypriot dialect, including terms and idioms that are specific to the island.

3. **Language in Turkish:**
    - The Turkish Cypriot community and those in Northern Cyprus speak Turkish as their first language. The local culture has an influence on the vernacular of Turkish Cypriots.

4. **Language in English:**
    - Since English is widely spoken and understood, both locals and visitors can communicate using it as a lingua franca. English is used in many meals, official papers, and road signs.

5. **Multicultural Community:**
    - Cyprus has a multilingual society as a result of its history of foreign influences. Particularly in tourist locations, you could run upon people who speak French, Russian, or other languages.

6. **Silhouettes:**
    - The deaf community in Cyprus uses Cypriot Sign Language, or CySL. It isn't as common as spoken languages, though.

7. **Etiquette in Communication:**
    - In general, Cypriots are kind and inviting. When you first get somewhere, it's polite to meet people

with a warm greeting and formal titles like "Mr." or "Mrs." until you're asked to use your first name.

8. Cultural Difference:
- Elder respect is important in Cypriot culture. It's customary to address elderly people with formality and respect.

9. Nonverbal Exchanges:
- The importance of nonverbal communication is shared by many Mediterranean civilizations. Cypriots can express emotions and meanings with their hands and faces.

10. Unity and Division of Languages:
- The political split between the Republic of Cyprus and the Turkish Republic of Northern Cyprus is reflected in the language differences on the island. It might be delicate to discuss language.

Gaining an understanding of Cyprus's linguistic diversity enhances the quality of your trip. This multilingual approach to communication enhances the island's history and culture, whether you're speaking Greek, Turkish, or English with the inhabitants.

Chapter 10

Relevant Information

For a hassle-free travel to Cyprus:

Work with the Euro (EUR).

Many people speak English.

Although not required, leaving a tip is appreciated.

See the prerequisites for a visa.

Honor regional traditions and manners.

Enjoy your visit!

Medical Attention and Emergencies

Cyprus is a safe and dependable travel destination since it provides excellent healthcare services. What you should know about Cyprus's emergency services and medical system is as follows:

1. **Medical Institutions:**
   - Cyprus offers both public and private healthcare services as part of a sophisticated healthcare system. Both locals and visitors can receive medical care at public hospitals, which also offer more upscale services.
2. **The EHIC, or European Health Insurance Card:**
   - During their visit, EU nationals can use their EHIC card to obtain the essential medical care. You can get the same medical care as residents with this card.
3. **Health Care Insurance:**
   - Travelers from outside the EU should have medical emergency coverage for their time in Cyprus through travel insurance.
4. **Safeguards:**
   - Although traveling to Cyprus is typically safe, it is still important to take common sense health measures like drinking plenty of water, applying sunscreen, and watching what you eat and drink.
5. **Prescriptions & Medication:**

- Bring enough of any prescribed drugs you need, along with a copy of your prescription, if any. Cyprus has most drugs, although it's advisable to bring extra supplies.

6. **Immunizations:**
- Before visiting Cyprus, find out whether there are any required vaccines. Speak with your local healthcare professional. For Europe, the recommended vaccine schedule is usually enough.

Cyprus provides emergency services and healthcare at a comforting level. In the event that medical attention is required, travelers can anticipate professional and timely emergency assistance. When traveling, it's always a good idea to be ready for everything that can come up and to keep up with the most recent health regulations.

Travel Advice and Safety

Cyprus is a lovely and friendly country to visit, but just like anywhere else, you should prioritize your safety and heed some travel advice to make the most of your trip. Here's how to make your trip memorable and safe:

1. Individual Security:
- Cyprus is a usually safe place to go. Still, it's a good idea to take the usual safety measures. Be mindful of your surroundings and keep a watch on your possessions, particularly in crowded situations.

2. Health Safety Measures:
- Use sunscreen, drink enough of water, and maintain good food and water hygiene to avoid common health problems associated with travel.

3. Local Ordinances and Rules:
- Learn about the laws and culture of the area. Cyprus has very severe laws against littering, smoking in public areas, and where you can and cannot drink alcohol.

4. Exchange of Currency:

- To exchange your currencies for euros, choose trustworthy banks or exchange bureaus. Do not exchange cash on the street.

5. **Moving:**
   - Getting a car rental is a common way to see the island. Use the left side of the road when driving. There is also public transportation available, including buses.

6. **Vehicle Safety:**
   - Cyprus has well-kept highways, but take extra care on the winding, narrow mountain roads. Wear seat belts and observe speed restrictions.

7. **Help for Emergencies:**
   - Keep the following emergency phone numbers on hand: 112 for general emergencies, 144 for medical help, 199 for law enforcement, and 140 for firefighters.

8. **Linguistic:**
   - Even though English is the primary language, locals may find it useful to know a few simple Greek or Turkish words.

9. Travel Protection:

- Travelers who are not from the EU should think about getting travel insurance that covers medical crises and other unforeseen circumstances.

10. Honor regional customs:

- Greek and Turkish Cypriots live in Cyprus among other varied communities. Respect regional traditions and customs, particularly when you are at places of worship.

11. Scenic Research:

- Cyprus has a lot of breathtaking scenery. Discover the breathtaking scenery, which includes the Troodos Mountains and immaculate beaches, but always remember to leave no mark.

12. Pouring Water:

- Cyprus's tap water is usually safe to drink, however bottled water is easily found if you'd like.

13. Time Zone:

- Cyprus uses Eastern European Summer Time (EEST) during daylight saving time and Eastern European Time (EET) during regular time.

You can make the most of your trip to Cyprus, a country renowned for its rich history, vibrant culture, and friendly people, by paying attention to these safety and travel advice. While being cautious and courteous, embrace the regional traditions, discover the scenery, and make lifelong memories.

Regional Laws and Traditions

To guarantee a courteous and pleasurable vacation, it's critical to be informed about the rules and traditions of the area before traveling to Cyprus. The following are important things to remember:

1. Trash and Tidying Up:
- There are strong anti-littering legislation in Cyprus. Don't leave litter in public areas and dispose of your rubbish in the appropriate bins.

2. Rules Regarding Smoking:

- There are designated smoking sites and it is not permitted to smoke in enclosed public settings. Respect others' feelings and obey no-smoking signs.

3. **Drinking of Alcohol:**
   - Cyprus has laws specifically prohibiting drinking in public places. It is best to consume alcoholic drinks in approved locations or in private.

4. **Cultural Intelligence:**
   - Greek and Turkish Cypriots live in Cyprus among other varied communities. Be mindful of regional traditions and customs, especially when visiting places of worship.

5. **Clothes Code:**
   - When visiting places of worship, such as churches and mosques, wear modest clothing. When necessary, take off your cap and cover your legs and shoulders.

6. **Still Life:**
   - Before taking a picture of someone, always get their permission, especially in isolated villages

and rural locations. There are locals who might rather not be photographed.

7. **Vernacular:**
   - Even though English is commonly spoken, it can improve your trip experience and be appreciated by locals if you try to acquire a few simple Greek or Turkish words.

8. **Honoring Seniors:**
   - Elder respect is very important in Cypriot society. It is normal to speak to senior people in a formal manner and with respect.

9. **Purchasing and haggling:**
   - While haggling over prices is uncommon in traditional retail establishments, it is possible in outdoor marketplaces or when interacting with street vendors.

10. **Safe Driving:**
    - Cyprus has well-kept highways, but take extra care on the winding, narrow mountain roads. Wear seat belts, observe speed limits, and refrain from using a phone while operating a vehicle.

11. **Preservation of the Environment:**

- The unspoiled beauty of Cyprus is a treasure. When visiting natural places, please respect the environment by not littering and by adhering to the established trails.

12. Gratuity:
- Tipping is not required, but it is appreciated. It is typical to tip servers in restaurants between 10% and 15% for good service.

13. Regional Food:
- Savor typical Cypriot fare like halloumi cheese, moussaka, and souvlaki. Saying "efharisto" (thank you) is a polite way to thank someone.

It is courteous to be aware of and abide by local rules and customs, as this improves your trip. With a little consideration for the island and its residents, you may make the most of your trip to Cyprus, a varied and culturally rich location.

Handy Expressions & Linguistic Advice

Even though English is commonly spoken in Cyprus, learning a few phrases from the locals will improve your trip and demonstrate your appreciation for their culture. Here's a guide to help you have productive conversations while there:

1. Salutations Basics:
- "Merhaba" in Turkish, "Geia sas" (Γειά σας) in Greek.
- "Kalimera" (Καλημέρα) is Greek for "good morning," and "Günaydın" in Turkish.
- "Kalispera" (Καλησπέρα) is Greek for "good evening," and "İyi akşamlar" is Turkish.

2. Empathizing Words:
- Please, "Lütfen" in Turkish, or "Parakalo" (Παρακαλώ) in Greek.
- "Efharisto" (Ευχαριστώ) in Greek, or "Teşekkür ederim" in Turkish, is said with gratitude.

- You are most welcome - "Rica ederim" in Turkish, or "Parakalo" (Παρακαλώ) in Greek.

3. **Typical Inquiries:**
   - Yes, "Evet" in Turkish or "Ne" (Ϝαι) in Greek.
   - No, it's "Hayır" in Turkish and "Ochi" (Όχι) in Greek.
   - Excuse me/sorry - "Üzgünüm" in Turkish, or "Signomi" (Συγνώμη) in Greek.

4. **Place Food Orders:**
   - "Menü, lütfen" in Turkish, or "Karta, parakalo" (Κάρτα, παρακαλώ) in Greek, is the menu, please.
   - Water is called "Su" in Turkish and "Nero" (Νερό) in Greek.
   - "Tha ithela..." (Θα ήθελα...) in Greek, or "İstiyorum..." in Turkish, is what I would like.

5. **Figures:**
   - When shopping or dining, it can be advantageous to know the numbers in the native tongue. For instance, "one" is "bir" in Turkish and "ena" (ένα) in Greek.

6. **Emergencies Words:**

- Assistance: "Yardım" in Turkish, or "Voithia" (Βοήθεια) in Greek.
- In Greek, "Xreiazomai ena giatro" (Χρειάζουι ένα γιατρό) means "I need a doctor," and in Turkish, "Bir doktora ihtiyacım var"

7. **Linguistic Advice:**
- Recognize the customs of the place by learning some simple salutations and courteous language.
- To facilitate communication, think about utilizing a translation app.
- English is used in many meals, official papers, and road signs.

Even though English is widely spoken in Cyprus, trying to speak a few local words will help you connect with the people and make the most of your trip. When foreigners express interest in their language and culture, the Cypriot people respond with warmth and gratitude.

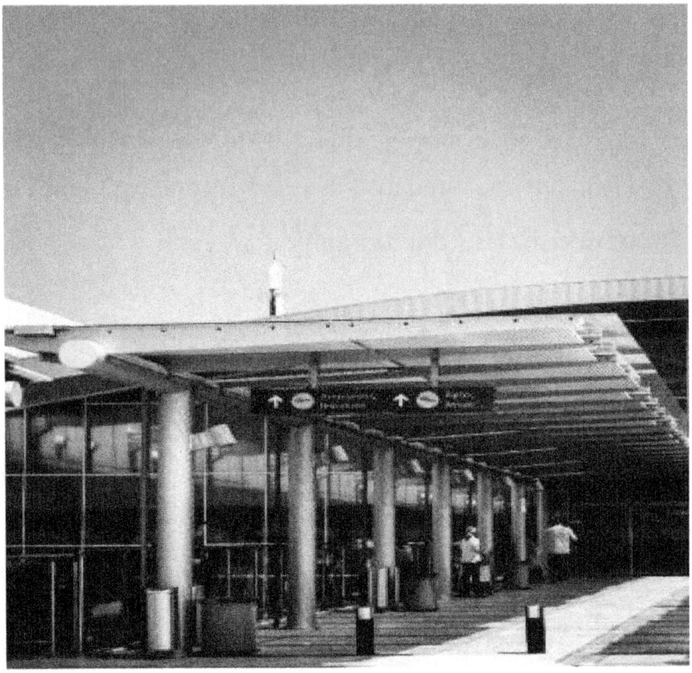

Chapter 11

Moving About

Easily explore Cyprus. You have three options: take public transportation, hire a cab, or rent a car. Because of the island's well-maintained road system, traveling about it is easy and pleasurable.

The Public Transit System

Public transportation in Cyprus is well-organized, making island exploration simple. What you should know about using buses and other public transportation to go about is as follows:

1. Buses:
- In Cyprus, buses are the main kind of public transportation. There is a vast transportation network on the island that links towns, cities, and well-known tourist attractions.

- The buses are a dependable form of transportation since they are often kept up and tidy. Check for bus timetables and stops at different areas, such as airports, well-known tourist destinations, and major city centers. Intercity Buses and Cyprus Public Transport (Cyprus by Bus) are the two primary bus companies operating on the island. Both provide routes that go around the whole island.
- The cost of tickets is affordable, and you may buy them straight from the bus driver. Remember that precise change is frequently needed. Intercity buses are an option for lengthier trips between cities. These provide air-conditioned, cozy transit choices.

2. Limassol - Nicosia - Larnaca Express Shuttle:
- The express shuttle service is useful if you're commuting between large cities like Nicosia, Larnaca, and Limassol. It offers a practical connection and is effective between these cities.

3. Taxicabs:

- In Cyprus, taxis are easily found. You can hail one at taxi stands or wave one down on the street. Although they cost more than buses, they offer a more convenient and adaptable mode of transportation. Use the taxi's meter and try to get a better deal on the fare in advance.

4. Railways:

- There aren't many trains in Cyprus, and they mostly go to Nicosia, the capital. In the future, train travel may become more accessible since the railway network is being updated and enlarged.

5. Ferries:

- Consider using a ferry if you intend to tour the islands and coastal areas off the coast of Cyprus. Frequent ferry services are available to connect several ports.

6. Strolling:

- Walking is a wonderful way to tour historic monuments, visit cafes, and learn about local culture in many of Cyprus's towns and cities, which are designed with pedestrians in mind.

7. **Scooters and ATVs for rent:**
   - All-terrain vehicles (ATVs) and scooter rentals are available in tourist regions as an alternate mode of transportation. Make sure you are aware of safety regulations and that you have the required permits.

8. **Tours with Guides:**
   - Whether by foot, by bicycle, or by bus, guided excursions offer a practical method to discover Cyprus's history, culture, and natural beauty while gaining local insight.

9. **Hiring a Vehicle:**
   - A lot of visitors choose to freely explore Cyprus by renting a car. Like in the UK, driving is done on the left side of the road on a well-maintained network of roads.

Using the public transportation system in Cyprus is a convenient method to explore the island's varied landscapes and natural beauties. While ferries and taxis offer more flexibility for more specialized travel needs, buses are a cheap and dependable mode of transportation. Take advantage of public transportation's convenience while taking in Cyprus' breathtaking scenery and vibrant culture.

Car Hire

Renting a car in Cyprus is an easy and adaptable way to see the island's many sights and landscapes. When thinking about renting a car in Cyprus, keep the following in mind:

1. Letting Companies:
- With locations at main airports and in well-known tourist spots like Larnaca, Paphos, and Limassol, Cyprus is home to a large number of automobile rental companies. Bookings can be made in advance or on-site.

2. Driving Permit:
- Generally, a valid driver's license from your home country is required in order to rent a car in Cyprus. Depending on your country, international driving permits may also be necessary.

3. Age Requirements:
- Although the minimum age may differ, most rental companies demand that drivers be at least 21 years old. For drivers under 25, certain agencies demand an extra cost.

4. Coverage:
- Insurance is typically provided for third-party liability when renting an automobile in Cyprus. For extra peace of mind, additional insurance choices are frequently offered, such as theft protection or collision damage waiver (also known as CDW).

5. Fuel Policy:
- Acquaint yourself with the rental agency's fuel policy. Certain firms supply a full tank of petrol and demand that you return the vehicle with the same amount of fuel, while others only charge for the first tank.

6. Rules for the Road:
- Like the UK, driving in Cyprus is done in the left hand. Learn about local driving laws, such as those pertaining to seat belt usage, speed

restrictions, and the use of cell phones while driving.

7. Parking:
- Be prepared to pay for parking in certain locations as parking might be difficult to find in urban regions. Avoid obstructing driveways and seek for parking spaces that are designated.

8. Type of Vehicle:
- From small cars to SUVs, you have a range of rental car options. Taking into account your intended route and the roads you intend to drive on can help you choose the right car size.

9. Reserving in advance:
- It's best to reserve your rental car well in advance to ensure you get the automobile of your choice, especially during the busiest travel times.

By giving you the freedom to explore the island's well-known attractions as well as its hidden gems, renting a car in Cyprus enables you to make the most of your trip. For a safe and comfortable ride, just make sure you comprehend the rental terms, traffic laws, and insurance alternatives.

Chapter 12

Taking Families and Kids on Vacation

Families are cordially invited to Cyprus. Take in the historical sites, family-friendly beaches, and welcoming, secure environment. A fantastic family holiday may be had there thanks to the child-friendly activities and facilities.

Activities Suitable for the Whole Family

Cyprus is a great place for families to travel because it has a lot of family-friendly attractions. Here are a few of the best family-friendly events and activities to check out:

1. Seashores:

- Many quiet, family-friendly beaches in Cyprus are ideal for swimming and water sports. Two particularly well-liked locations are Fig Tree Bay in Protaras and Coral Bay in Paphos.

2. **Amusement Parks:**
   - With their wave pools, waterslides, and other attractions, water parks like WaterWorld Waterpark in Ayia Napa and Fasouri Watermania in Limassol offer an exciting day of fun.

3. **Zoo in Pafos:**
   - For those who love animals, there's also the Pafos Zoo in Paphos. A variety of animals, including crocodiles and giraffes, call it home.

4. **Historic Sites:**
   - Archaeological monuments like the Tombs of the Kings in Paphos and the ancient city of Kourion near Limassol showcase the rich history of Cyprus. Together, explore these historical gems.

5. **The Adventure Parks:**
   - The island has adventure parks, such as Camel Park in Mazotos, where children may ride camels

and engage with animals in a tranquil environment.

6. **Outdoor pursuits:**
   - Savor outdoor experiences like horseback riding, trekking in the Troodos Mountains, and exploring environmental reserves like Cape Greco National Forest Park.

7. **Resorts That Are Family Friendly:**
   - With kid-friendly clubs, entertainment, and daycare available, many resorts in Cyprus cater to families, allowing parents to unwind while their kids have a good time.

8. **Regional Foods:**
   - Taste the variety of Cypriot food, which includes mouthwatering sweets like loukoumades and classic meze. Child-friendly menus are available at many establishments.

9. **Cultural Encounters:**
   - Attend village festivals with your family to introduce them to the customs of the area and enjoy local cuisine, music, and dance.

10. **Open-air markets:**

- Introduce your kids to fresh vegetables and locally made crafts by exploring local markets, such as the Cyprus Land Farmers' Market.

For families, Cyprus offers the ideal fusion of historical sites, scenic landscapes, and outdoor activities.

Health and Child Care Services

In Cyprus, you may anticipate having access to first-rate medical care and child care while traveling with kids.

What you need know to protect your family's welfare is as follows:

Daycare Providers

Hotels and Resorts:
- A lot of Cyprus's family-friendly hotels and resorts provide childcare options, such as kids' clubs and supervised play areas. These programs let parents spend quality time alone with their kids while they're having a good time.

Private Babysitters:
- You can make arrangements for private babysitters by contacting respectable

organizations or by requesting suggestions from your lodging. Make sure the nanny has references and expertise.

Hospitals and Clinics:
- If your child needs medical attention, Cyprus has both public and private, well-equipped hospitals and clinics. They offer emergency services as well as pediatric treatment.

Pharmacies:
- They are easily accessible, and pharmacists can offer advice on common pediatric illnesses as well as over-the-counter drugs. Find out the closest drugstore by asking a local or at your lodging.

Emergency Services:
- To request general assistance or an ambulance in the event of a medical emergency, dial 112 or 144. Cyprus's emergency response system is dependable.

Health Insurance:

- If you are going overseas, you should think about getting travel insurance that includes coverage for medical costs, including those for your child. Don't forget to bring the required insurance paperwork.

Cyprus is a family-friendly vacation spot where you can anticipate amenities and services geared toward your kids' wellbeing.

Chapter 13

Outdoor Excursions

Hiking, riding, and water activities are great ways to explore the breathtaking scenery of Cyprus. This lovely island offers outdoor adventures for anyone to enjoy, from the Troodos Mountains to seaside delights.

Snorkeling and Scuba Pursuit

For those who love the water, Cyprus is a fascinating location because it provides excellent options for both snorkeling and scuba diving. To fully explore the island's breathtaking underwater world, be aware of the following information:

Diving for Scuba

With a wide variety of diving locations appropriate for novices and experts alike, Cyprus offers crystal-clear, mild waters. Cape Greco Marine Park, the Zenobia wreck near Larnaca, and the Akamas Peninsula are popular dive sites. Divers seeking certification classes and guided dives have access to an array of dive shops and schools. Explore the diverse marine ecosystem, which includes colorful fish, octopuses, and in some places, turtles, by exploring underwater caves, reefs, and other habitats.

Snorkeling

Without the need for specialized training or equipment, snorkeling is an excellent way to enjoy Cyprus's underwater beauty.

With their pristine waters and abundant marine life just a few steps from the coast, several beaches and coves, such Konnos Bay and Nissi Beach, are ideal for snorkeling.

Narrated Tours

If diving or snorkeling is something you have never done before, think about signing up for a guided tour. The greatest locations and information about the local marine environment can be found with the assistance of knowledgeable guides.

Conserving and staying safe

Don't touch or harm coral reefs or marine life out of respect for them and the environment. Dive to the depth of your ability and observe safety precautions. Undiscovered treasures can be found in Cyprus's undersea environment. Explore the island's amazing variety of marine life and underwater scenery, whether you're a licensed diver or just searching for a relaxing snorkeling experience.

Using a Kite and Windsurfer

With its steady winds and breathtaking coastline, Cyprus is a dream destination for those who enjoy windsurfing and kitesurfing. The following information will help you enjoy these thrilling water sports on the island:

A wind-surfer:
- Cyprus's southern coast is a popular place to windsurf, especially in places like Larnaca and

Pissouri, where you can find windsurfing schools and facilities.
- The summer months bring regular blows of the Meltemi wind, which makes windsurfing ideal. While more experienced surfers can rent equipment and tackle the waves, beginners can enroll in classes.

Using a kite:
- Cyprus is a great place to go kitesurfing, with amazing locations including Paramali Beach and Lady's Mile Beach near Limassol.
- The best months to go kitesurfing on the island are May through October, when the wind is at its best. Many of these places also have kitesurfing schools and rental options.

Tools and Instructions:
- The many kitesurfing and windsurfing centers rent out equipment, or you can bring your own.

- Beginners can enroll in classes with knowledgeable teachers who will go over the fundamentals of controlling the kite or board as well as providing safety instructions.

Security and Protocols:
- Always abide by the rules of safety and use the appropriate gear, such as life jackets and harnesses.
- Swimmers, other water sports enthusiasts, and any areas that are restricted should all be observed.
- Prior to leaving, check the local wind conditions and forecasts; never venture outside of your comfort zone.

Natural Beauty:
- In addition to the excitement of the sports, you'll be treated to amazing shoreline views and glistening waves, which will provide an unforgettable backdrop for your windsurfing and kitesurfing excursions.

With its steady winds, warm waters, and gorgeous beaches, Cyprus offers the ideal playground for experienced windsurfers and kitesurfers as well as novices wishing to attempt these thrilling sports. It's an amazing adventure that blends the natural beauty of the island with adventure.

Hiking and Climbing Rocks

With its breathtaking scenery, rock climbing and hiking are two of the many outdoor activities available in Cyprus. To start these daring activities, you should be aware of the following:

Rock ascent

Cyprus is gaining popularity as a rock climbing destination because of its limestone cliffs and other natural structures. A variety of climbing routes appropriate for different ability levels may be found at well-known rock climbing locations such as the Avakas Gorge, Cape Greco, and Stavrovouni. Climbing gyms and guides are available to assist you take full use of the rocky landscape on the island, regardless of your level of experience.

Make sure all the gear is ready for the climb, such as helmets, harnesses, and ropes. Observe safety precautions and climb to your ability level.

Climbing

Cyprus is a great place to go hiking because of its varied topography, which includes paths through verdant forests, craggy mountains, and along gorgeous coasts. Hiking destinations that are captivating to explore include the Troodos Mountains, the Akamas Peninsula, and the Cedar Valley. The level of hiking trails varies, ranging from family-friendly strolls to strenuous paths for more experienced hikers. Make sure you are ready by dressing appropriately for hiking, packing supplies like water, food, and a map, and researching the weather before you go.

Lead Envoys

Joining guided rock climbing or hiking tours can improve your experience and teach you about the history, flora, and animals of the area. Expert guides can offer you advice on the best routes and insights into the island's scenic surroundings.

Preservation and Deference

The breathtaking natural beauty of Cyprus should be protected. Take your waste with you, protect wildlife and plant life, and always abide by the Leave No Trace philosophy.

Cyprus provides a world of adventure for rock climbers and hikers, whether you're ascending limestone cliffs or hiking through ancient woods. For those looking for an active and natural getaway, the island is a tempting destination because of its rich biodiversity and different landscapes.

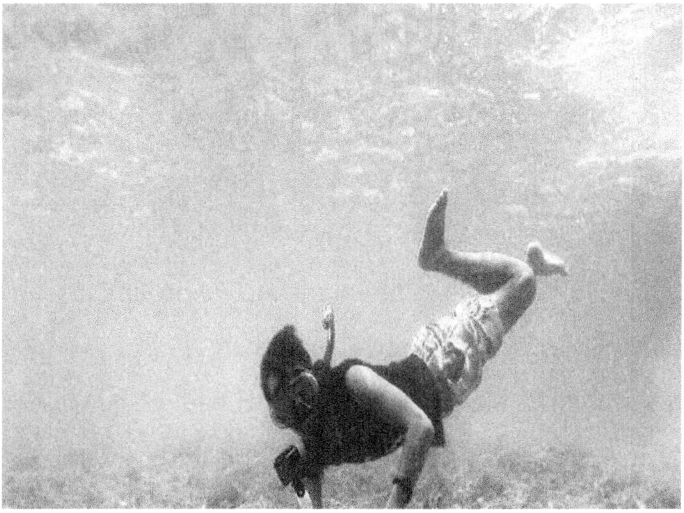

Chapter 14

Traveling With Caution

Respect the island's communities, environment, and culture while having a great time there. Leave no trace, patronize small businesses, and travel with consideration to protect Cyprus' natural beauty for future generations.

Greenhouse Gas Initiatives

Cyprus has made notable progress toward sustainability and environmental conservation. The island's principal projects and endeavors are as follows:

Park on the Akamas Peninsula:

- Nesting sea turtles and unusual orchids can be found among the rich flora and animals of the protected Akamas Peninsula. To protect its natural beauty, conservation measures are in place.

Conserving Marine Life:

- Cyprus firmly believes in safeguarding its maritime environments. Among the initiatives are the tracking and defense of sea turtles, including loggerhead and green turtles, that are nesting.

Sustainable Energy:
- To lessen its carbon footprint and dependency on fossil fuels, Cyprus has made investments in renewable energy sources like wind farms and solar power.

Management of Waste:
- In order to lessen landfill waste and encourage environmentally friendly habits, the island is enhancing its waste management and recycling initiatives.

Reserves and National Parks:
- To protect its biodiversity and natural landscapes, Cyprus has created a number of national parks and nature reserves, such as the Troodos National Forest Park.

Knowledge and Consciousness:
- The goal of environmental education projects and programs is to increase locals' and tourists'

knowledge of sustainable practices, wildlife preservation, and conservation.

Traveling responsibly:

- Sustainable and ethical practices, such as eco-friendly lodging and eco-tours, are becoming more and more important to Cyprus' tourism sector.

Travelers may help ongoing efforts to preserve Cyprus's natural environment and advance a more sustainable and responsible approach to the island's tourism industry by taking part in these activities and encouraging eco-friendly practices.

Conscientious Travel Approaches

With an emphasis on protecting its natural beauty, cultural legacy, and local people, Cyprus is dedicated to responsible tourism. During your visit, keep the following important procedures in mind:

1. Eco-friendly Housing:
- Select environmentally friendly lodgings that reduce waste, use less water, and use less electricity.

2. Show Nature Respect:
- While visiting beaches, natural reserves, and other protected areas, abide by the "Leave No Trace" philosophy. Take your rubbish with you, stay on trails that are designated, and don't disturb any wildlife.

3. Encourage regional companies:
- For genuine experiences and to support the local economy, choose locally owned eateries, stores, and excursions.

4. Respect for Culture:
- When you visit historical landmarks, mosques, and churches, treat them with respect. Observe the norms and regulations established by these websites and dress modestly when necessary.

5. Use Less Plastic:

- Bring a reusable shopping bag and water bottle to reduce plastic waste. In Cyprus, a lot of companies are attempting to cut back on single-use plastics.

6. Protection of Wildlife:
- Find out about and lend your support to wildlife conservation projects, especially those that conserve sea turtles around coastal areas.

7. Conscientious Use of Water:
- There are dry spells in Cyprus, so be mindful of the water you consume when showering and eating.

8. Conscientious Cycling and Hiking:
- Respect local species, stay on approved pathways, and follow the rules regarding water sports and rock climbing.

9. Reusing:
- Cyprus is working to enhance its recycling initiatives. Utilizing recycling bins and correctly sorting your waste will help.

10. Get Knowledge:

- Discover the local customs and environmental and cultural legacy of Cyprus. Part of ethical tourism involves getting to know the locals and showing respect for their way of life.

You may support the sustainability of Cyprus and the welfare of its communities and natural beauty by adopting responsible tourist practices.

Chapter 15

Emergency Contacts and Resources

Remember to dial 112 for all emergencies in Cyprus. For specific needs, consult local authorities, hospitals, or your embassy. Stay safe during your stay!

Value-Added Phone Numbers

For your comfort and safety while visiting Cyprus, it is imperative that you have access to important phone numbers. The following figures are crucial to remember:

1. General Emergencies:
- For fast assistance in the event of a police, fire, or medical emergency, dial 112. Cyprus's general emergency number is this.

2. **Police:**
   - Call your local police station to report a small incident or for non-emergency police help. In an emergency, dial 112 for general emergencies.
3. **Medical Emergencies:**
   - Dial an ambulance if you experience a medical emergency. You can get in contact with the proper medical services by calling 112, the general emergency number.
4. **Hospitals and Clinics:**
   - Learn the contact details for the medical facilities in the vicinity where you are staying. The General Hospitals in Nicosia, Limassol, and Larnaca are a few of the major medical facilities.

5. **Pharmacies:**
   - The pharmacy industry in Cyprus is well-established. To get medical advice and medications, find the one that is closest to your location.
6. **Lost or Stolen Items:**

- In the event that anything is lost or stolen, get in touch with the local police station. This includes passports. In such cases, advice can also be obtained via your embassy or consulate.

7. **Language support:**
- Even though English is the primary language of Cyprus, it can be beneficial to have access to translation services or language support, particularly in non-tourist areas.

It can help you feel more secure and make sure you have the resources you need in case of emergencies or other problems when visiting Cyprus if you have these phone numbers on hand.

Missions Abroad and Consulates

When visiting Cyprus from another country, it's critical to know the addresses and phone numbers of your home nation's embassy or consulate in Cyprus. These diplomatic posts can help you in a variety of circumstances and offer crucial services to residents of other countries:

1. Consulates versus embassies:
- The main diplomatic representative of a nation in Cyprus is an embassy, which is normally housed in Nicosia, the capital. It deals with many different diplomatic issues.
- A consulate is a division of an embassy and is frequently located in large cities such as Paphos or Limassol. Consulates are primarily concerned with offering consular services to people, which include help with legal, visa, and passport-related concerns.

2. Offerings of Services:
- Assistance with lost or stolen passports, emergency travel documents, legal and notary services, and support during catastrophes or crises are just a few of the services provided by embassies and consulates.

- In addition to helping with communication with local officials and providing information on laws and regulations in the area, they can also provide advice on healthcare and medical situations.

3. **How to Get in Touch:**
   - Note down the address, phone number, and email of your nation's embassy or consulate in Cyprus prior to your journey.
   - For usage in an emergency, a lot of embassies and consulates also feature emergency phone lines or contact information after hours.

4. **Sign-up:**
   - When visiting Cyprus for an extended period of time, some embassies or consulates can advise visitors to register. Getting updates on local conditions or staying in touch in an emergency might both benefit from this.

5. **International Embassies:**

- Embassies and consulates from a number of nations are located in Cyprus, making multilingual help available.

It's wise to have this information on hand when you travel, particularly if you'll be in Cyprus for business, education, or other reasons and won't be staying for a long time. In the event that you run into problems while visiting Cyprus, the embassy or consulate of your home nation can offer you invaluable assistance.

Healthcare Institutions

Cyprus has a sophisticated healthcare system with a variety of medical facilities to guarantee the health of both locals and guests. What you should know about Cyprus's medical services is as follows:

1. Clinics and Hospitals:
- In Cyprus, there are both public and private healthcare facilities. The main public healthcare facilities are found in Nicosia, Limassol, and Larnaca. Comprehensive medical services,

including emergency treatment, are provided by these hospitals.
- Private medical facilities, such the Mediterranean Hospital in Limassol and the American Medical Center in Nicosia, are well-known for their personnel that speaks English and provides excellent medical care.

2. **Health Care Practitioners:**
- Cyprus boasts a highly proficient medical workforce, with numerous globally trained physicians and healthcare practitioners.
- Medical professionals, including specialists and general practitioners (GPs), are easily accessible to offer a comprehensive range of medical services.

3. **Drugstores:**
- In Cyprus, pharmacies are widespread, and their services include dispensing over-the-counter drugs and providing medical advice. If you require non-prescription medications or health information, choose the pharmacy that is closest to your location.

4. **Health Travel:**
   - Cyprus has been a popular destination for medical tourism, especially with regard to cosmetic surgery and elective procedures. Patients seeking top-notch medical care on the island come from a variety of nations.

5. **Communication and Language:**
   - In Cyprus, many people who work in the medical field speak English. The fluency of medical practitioners in English, particularly in tourist locations, facilitates easy communication of healthcare needs by English-speaking visitors.

6. **Health Benefits:**
   - It's a good idea to obtain health and medical expense coverage for your trip insurance when visiting Cyprus. Keep the required insurance paperwork on you at all times.

7. **Help for Emergencies:**
   - In Cyprus, 112 is the global emergency number to call for quick medical assistance in case of an

emergency. This will put you in contact with ambulances and medical services.

Cyprus's healthcare institutions provide top-notch services and attention. The island's healthcare system is prepared to guarantee your wellbeing while you're visiting, whether you need normal care or find yourself in an emergency.

Chapter 16

Addenda

Respect the culture of Cyprus, enjoy the cuisine, and establish communication with simple words and phrases. Prioritize your health, investigate a variety of transportation alternatives, and find hidden jewels. Take part in local celebrations, be mindful of the environment, and prepare for inclement weather. Record memories in an appropriate manner. Have fun on your trip to Cyprus!

Maps and Schedules of Transportation

Maps and transit schedules make it easier to navigate Cyprus. These resources can help you in the following ways while you're here:

Maps

Cyprus maps are widely accessible and come in a variety of media, such as paper maps, digital maps, and GPS navigation systems. Free maps are available at airports, visitor centers, and rental car companies. Maps are useful for exploring cities, locating lodging, and locating tourist sites. For road vacations and adventures, particularly in rural areas, detailed road maps are invaluable. Real-time navigation is available via smartphone apps such as Google Maps and online map services, which can also assist with route planning and time estimation.

Schedules for Transportation:

Buses that link Cyprus's main cities and towns are part of the well-run public transportation network. Bus route timetables are accessible via mobile apps, the internet, and bus stops. For people who are interested in traveling between cities, the Cyprus State Railway also provides train timetables. Ferry schedules for adjacent islands, like Greece or Turkey, can be found online or at ports. Airport transportation schedules and information on vehicle rentals are supplied by car rental companies.

Whether you're traveling around the island's scenic landscapes, exploring towns, or seeking adventure in the outdoors, maps and transportation schedules are essential tools for organizing your travels. They facilitate your mobility and allow you to fully enjoy your stay in Cyprus.

Linguistic Translation Reference

Being a multilingual place like Cyprus, having a language translation guide can make your trip even more enjoyable. It can help you in the following ways while you're there:

1. Multilingual Setting:
- Greek and Turkish are the official languages of the bilingual nation of Cyprus. Nonetheless, English is commonly spoken, particularly in tourist destinations. A translation guide can assist in bridging linguistic divides.

2. Key Expressions:

- Common words and expressions that are useful for daily interactions are usually included in language translation guides. This includes introducing oneself, requesting directions, placing meal orders, and more.

3. **Respect for Cultural Differences:**
    - You can show respect for the local way of life and improve your communication with Cypriots by learning and utilizing a few phrases in the native tongue, such as "Kalimera" (Greek for "Good morning").

4. **Using the Menus:**
    - When choosing food at a restaurant, especially if the menu isn't in English, a translation guide might be quite helpful. It's a helpful tool for learning about the regional food.

5. **Situations of Emergency:**
    - Despite the fact that many Cypriots are English speakers, having a translation guide can be quite helpful when contacting local authorities for assistance or in an emergency.

6. Diversity of Languages:
- Because Cyprus is a heterogeneous country, you can hear people speaking Arabic or Russian, particularly in regions where there are a lot of expats.

During your trip to Cyprus, a language translation guide might prove to be an invaluable ally for language enthusiasts hoping to converse with locals or anyone looking for useful communication tools.

Chapter 17

Index

Your go-to resource for fast information retrieval is the index in your travel guide to Cyprus. It makes it simple to locate particular information, locations, or topics inside the guide by listing keywords, places, and topics along with the relevant page numbers. For effective navigation and a deeper comprehension of the stunning island of Cyprus, this index is your go-to resource.

Instantaneous Keyword Index

One extremely useful tool in your Cyprus travel guide to improve your trip is the Keyword Index. It serves as a thorough directory, listing crucial words, keywords, and themes along with the relevant page references, giving readers a clear path for speedy information retrieval. This priceless tool can accompany you on your travels in the following ways:

1. **Effective Navigation:**
   - The Keyword Index is a useful tool for rapidly locating certain facts or information. It helps you find the stuff you're looking for precisely by saving you the time and effort of turning pages.
2. **Extensive Coverage:**
   - The Keyword Index includes a broad range of topics, from historical landmarks and tourist destinations to useful knowledge like regional laws and customs. This index covers every aspect of your journey that you may be interested in.
3. **Customized Discovery:**
   - What types of historical locations, outdoor activities, or gourmet experiences appeal to you? You can find a plethora of material to customize your research based on your interests by just consulting the pertinent keywords in the index.
4. **Improved Comprehension:**
   - The Keyword Index provides you with the knowledge you need for a more rewarding trip, whether you're looking for background on a

specific place or attempting to grasp the local way of life.

5. **Quick reference:**
- This index is your best buddy if you need answers quickly and are on the go. It gives you fast access to the necessary knowledge, much like having an informed local guide at your fingertips.

The Keyword Index is a trustworthy compass that will help you easily explore the huge terrain of information that the Cyprus travel guide offers. This lovely island awaits you. It guarantees that you get the most out of your trip to Cyprus and is a potent tool for effective exploration.

Conclusion

As your journey through the enchanting landscapes and cultural treasures of Cyprus draws to a close, the island's allure lingers in the echoes of its rich history, the embrace of its azure shores, and the warmth of its vibrant communities. In the tapestry of Cyprus, where ancient mythology meets modernity, you've unearthed the secrets of its archaeological wonders, traversed sun-kissed beaches, and indulged in the tantalizing flavors of its cuisine.

From the mystical allure of Paphos, steeped in mythology and archaeological wonders, to the vibrant coastal city of Limassol pulsating with life, each corner of Cyprus has woven a story that resonates with the heartbeat of the Mediterranean. The trove of history hidden within the UNESCO-listed sites, including the awe-inspiring ancient city of Kourion and the medieval charm of Bellapais Abbey, paints a vivid picture of Cyprus as a living testament to time's passage.

The journey into the Troodos Mountains has revealed the island's untamed beauty, where quaint villages and Byzantine churches perch amid pine-scented landscapes. As you descended to the coastal plains, the mesmerizing beaches of Ayia Napa and Protaras unfolded, inviting you to surrender to the crystal-clear waters and embrace the laid-back rhythm of island life.

Cyprus, a culinary haven, has tantalized your taste buds with meze feasts, freshly caught seafood, and the sweet notes of Cypriot wine. The traditional villages, each with its unique character, have welcomed you with open arms, inviting you to partake in the warmth of Cypriot hospitality and savor the simplicity of authentic island life.

In the cities, whether it's the bustling energy of Nicosia, where history and modernity coalesce, or the coastal charm of Larnaca with its picturesque salt lake, Cyprus has unfolded as a mosaic of experiences. The vibrant street art, lively festivals, and the intoxicating aroma of freshly brewed Cyprus coffee have added layers to the cultural tapestry of this Mediterranean gem.

As you bid farewell to Cyprus, the memories forged amid its sunlit landscapes, ancient ruins, and welcoming communities become the treasure trove of experiences that accompany you. Whether you sought relaxation on pristine beaches, embarked on historical quests, or simply revealed the island's culinary delights, Cyprus has left an indelible mark on your heart.

In the glow of Cyprus's sunsets, where hues of orange and pink dance on the horizon, you carry not just a travelog but a profound connection to a destination that transcends time. Cyprus, with its timeless charm and contemporary spirit, beckons you to return, promising that each visit will unravel new facets of its allure. As you journey onward, Cyprus remains not just a place on the map but a mosaic of memories etched in your wanderlust-filled heart, a testament to the astonishing beauty and cultural richness of this Mediterranean jewel.

Printed in Great Britain
by Amazon